Praise for *Cop Under Fire*

"Sheriff David Clarke has truly moved beyond race and politics, which allows him to look through the reality prism of crime in America. He is an 'America First' law enforcement officer and one of the finest and stalwart gentlemen I've ever met. Sheriff Clarke understands our Constitution and knows what to do to restore civility to our country. Respect for the law and its enforcement is his badge of honor. Every citizen must read this book!"

—**Paul E. Vallely**, Major General, US Army (Ret)
Chairman, Stand Up America/Glacial Forum,
Chairman, Legacy National Security Advisory Group,
and Chairman, Syrian Liaison Group

"At a time when too many leaders value political correctness above honest discussion, Sheriff David Clarke provides a much-needed voice of reason in tackling America's challenges. He speaks his mind, and his no-nonsense approach to law and order is exactly what we need to make our country safer. Clarke knows that criminals commit crimes—not guns. His commitment to protecting law-abiding gun owners while getting criminals off the street is a model for all leaders."

—**Chris W. Cox**
Executive Director, NRA Institute for Legislative Action

"Sheriff David Clarke is an American hero, and a powerful voice against the racist radicals who have declared war on our police. Sheriff Clarke understands the radical nature of this movement and the threat it poses to the frontline defenders of our communities, and especially our inner-city communities. We owe him a debt of gratitude for standing up to the haters and destroyers, and for speaking the truth. We owe it to ourselves to read this brave book and arm ourselves for the battles ahead."

—**David Horowitz**
Author, Political Analyst, and
Founder of the David Horowitz Freedom Center

"The media and political establishment in my community is obsessed with silencing Sheriff David Clarke because his message threatens their culture of entitlement, excuse making, and race hustling. Sheriff Clarke doesn't back down because the people have his back. Even in a predominantly liberal community, his message of law and order, accountability, and self-empowerment resonates. He is one of America's most important cultural voices.

—**Mark Belling**
Talk Radio Host for 1130 WISN-AM in Milwaukee and
Columnist for Newspapers Including the *Milwaukee Post*

"At a time when America seems to have lost its way, Sheriff David Clarke offers critically important leadership, both as one of the nation's top cops and as a much-needed public truth teller. His no-nonsense approach to law enforcement and unwavering sense of moral clarity are invaluable as we begin to restore our foundational principles and bring this exceptional nation back to full strength. A must-read."

—**Monica Crowley**, Ph.D.
Fox News Channel,
The Washington Times

"If you have already encountered David Clarke in action—whether knocking the stuffing out of a supercilious TV news anchor or delivering a clarion defense of law and order at the Republican National Convention—you will feel right at home with this rousing survey of the present American scene. If, however, this is your first—and, sadly, belated—exposure to Sheriff Clarke, be prepared for the ride of your life. Clarke is a unique voice today: fearless in his contempt for political correctness and eloquent in his articulation of core American values. There is no more influential spokesman for the police; he has fought back relentlessly against the dangerous lies spread by the Black Lives Matter movement. In *Cop Under Fire*, Clarke takes on the social destruction wrought by the liberal crusade against personal responsibility. He movingly recounts his disciplined upbringing, providing a model of the only solution to urban dysfunction that can possibly succeed: committed, responsible parents. Clarke's clashes with the Democratic political machine in Milwaukee are a lesson in *true* democratic values, based on responsiveness to public needs. One can only hope that the fortuitous timing of *Cop Under Fire*, coming as the country embarks on a radically new presidential administration, is a sign that the era of delusional victimology and identity politics is coming to an end."

—Heather Mac Donald
Thomas W. Smith Fellow at the Manhattan Institute
and Author of *The War on Cops*

"My mother once told me, 'Someday, everybody has to sit on their own bottom.' That's a message Sheriff Clarke addresses so personally and eloquently with this book. If America listens and learns, we'll be a better nation for it, and certainly a more united one."

—T. Boone Pickens
Chairman/CEO of BP Capital

"I have had the pleasure of getting to know Sheriff David Clarke over the past twelve months. Over this short time period, Sheriff Clarke has shown that he is a man of tremendous character who exemplifies honesty and integrity. His beliefs are based not only in academia but also real-world, personal experiences, which makes his words invaluable. He does not put political affiliation, race, or gender before his patriotism for the great nation—this in itself gives him immense credibility and exemplifies leadership. I implore all to read *Cop Under Fire*, because Sheriff Clarke's personal first-hand experiences will provide all with a better example of racism, its causes, and how the liberal Left continues to use it for their agenda at the expense of police officers' lives. Sheriff Clarke is a tremendous leader, follower, and a strong voice of reason who needs to be heard by all!"

—Kris "Tanto" Paronto
Former Ranger (2nd Battalion, 75th Regiment),
Security and Military Consultant, and
Hero of Benghazi Attack

"*Cop Under Fire* is a revealing narrative by an experienced law enforcement officer who understands both the cultural clashes that are occurring in American society and the public safety concerns of the average, hard-working, law-abiding American—no matter their color. Sheriff Clarke's rejection of the identity politics that are being used to divide our nation and his dedication to telling the truth makes him the kind of honorable, principled public official we see all too little of these days."

—**Hans A. von Spakovsky**
Senior Legal Fellow, The Heritage Foundation,
and Former U.S. Justice Department Official

COP UNDER
FIRE

MOVING BEYOND HASHTAGS OF RACE, CRIME & POLITICS
FOR A BETTER AMERICA

SHERIFF DAVID CLARKE JR.

WITH NANCY FRENCH

WORTHY®
PUBLISHING

Published by Worthy Books, an imprint of Worthy Publishing Group, a division of Worthy Media, Inc., One Franklin Park, 6100 Tower Circle, Suite 210, Franklin, TN 37067.

WORTHY is a registered trademark of Worthy Media, Inc.

HELPING PEOPLE EXPERIENCE THE HEART OF GOD

eBook available wherever digital books are sold.
Audiobook available from Oasis Audio.

Library of Congress Control Number: 2016961620

Cover photo: Sheriff David Clarke speaking at the 2016 Conservative Political Action Conference (CPAC) in National Harbor, Maryland. This work is licensed under a Creative Commons Attribution 2.0 Generic License. It is attributed to Gage Skidmore, and the original version can be found at https://www.flickr.com/photos/gageskidmore/24951347433/.
Author photo: Barry Morgenstein Photography, www.BarryMorgenstein.com

For foreign and subsidiary rights, contact rights@worthypublishing.com

Published in association with the literary agency of Legacy LLC, Winter Park, Florida 32789.

ISBN: 978-1617958571 (hardcover)

Printed in the United States of America

17 18 19 20 21 LBM 8 7 6 5 4 3 2 1

*To the men and women who are privileged
to wear the badge and uniform of their local community
and, while serving and protecting, put themselves
in harm's way . . . and to the proud profession of policing
that has been a part of my life for nearly four decades.*

CONTENTS

FOREWORD

by Sean Hannity

I FIRST MET SHERIFF DAVID CLARKE when he came on my show to talk politics, but I immediately knew he wasn't like many of the other conservatives I'd ever met. Sheriff Clarke, with this cowboy hat and boots, doesn't look like your typical Wisconsin resident. In fact, he looks like a sheriff out of an old wild west movie. He's a man with honor and courage, values that are more common in those old films than in pop culture these days.

That's why I love *Cop Under Fire: Moving Beyond Hashtags of Race, Crime, and Politics for a Better America*. It's about a man from the Milwaukee projects who thrived amidst challenging circumstances, who overcame racial politics in the police department, and who rose to the office of Milwaukee County Sheriff. It's about a man who dared to call out America's first black president for his lies, corruption, and disregard for the constitutional process. It's about a man who runs and was elected as a Democrat, but instead of buying into the modern liberalism dogma of the Left, he chooses to live by his principles and force the Democrat Party to excommunicate him if they don't like it.

David Clarke refuses to bow a knee to political correctness, and he refuses to give his party over to the kinds of black activists whose policies would destroy America. That's why I have Sheriff Clarke on my show so frequently: he says things you need to hear. Some viewers don't like his straightforward approach, thinking that he's too blunt or not sufficiently "tolerant." In fact, some of my colleagues at Fox have said he is too controversial. But I keep inviting him back because he says important things, usually, in the most memorable way possible.

Apparently, America agrees with me: it's time for some straight talk.

I think Sheriff Clarke makes people uneasy because he defies easy categorization. He's black, but he's against Black Lives Matter. He ran as a Democrat in Milwaukee, but he spoke at the Republican National Convention. He's from an urban area but he's more conservative than an Alabama tea party member. It's easier for people to stereotype than to deal with the actual man and his actual beliefs. That's why you hear people criticizing the man but rarely criticizing the substance of his arguments.

That's why I like the guy. As many of you know, I was born in New York City. I've also raised eyebrows by saying that I'm a "registered Conservative" and not a Republican—though people often mistake me for one. While some people believe that "conservatism" only thrives in rural areas, I love seeing people like Sheriff Clarke who hails from an area not typically known for producing conservatives. Isn't it time to think beyond the old categories of Republicans and Democrats? People who live in the real, complicated world tend to learn really fast what works and what doesn't—no matter where they live or what color their skin. And reality teaches lessons in conservatism.

For Sheriff Clarke, those lessons have been hard won.

Remember when the election of Barack Obama was supposed to signal the end of race issues in America? Well, that hasn't happened, has it—and some bad racial moments have happened in Milwaukee. In spite of President Obama's eight-year term—or maybe because of it—this nation is more divided than ever on issues of color. How we can rise above our current division to once again be a truly united people in pursuit of liberty and justice for all?

In this book, Sheriff Clarke writes about the lessons he's learned over the course of his thirty-eight years of law enforcement and shows once again that he's a true American. He writes about how his traditional upbringing in the housing projects of Milwaukee improbably molded him into the cowboy-hat-and-boot-wearing sheriff we know and love today. He tells about why he recorded a public service announcement in 2013 in which he told residents of his county that they needed to play a role in defending themselves and their families, explaining that self-protection is not something to be outsourced to the government and encouraging citizens to consider taking a firearm safety course. This caused liberals all over America to foam at the mouth, even though the Second Amendment has been alive and well since it was ratified in 1791.

He also reveals the hard, ugly truth behind "Black LIES Matter" (as he likes to call them), which will forever change the way you look at this nefarious political movement. In one particularly chilling chapter, he explains why he thinks this movement should be called a terrorist organization . . . and I defy you to disagree once you hear his reasoning.

But this book is not all gloom and doom, focusing on how bad things are in this nation. To the contrary, Sheriff Clarke presents interesting solutions to problems that have plagued us for decades. He even explains how "we the people" can wrest power away from a federal government too eager to wield its authority and bully anyone with whom they disagree politically. Plus, he talks about a constitutional solution to government overreach that should make both liberals and conservatives happy.

Here's the truth: the principles Sheriff Clarke stands for are the same principles this nation was built on. He's much more than the

Milwaukee County Sheriff. He's America's Sheriff . . . and *Cop Under Fire* is must-reading for people who love this great country. In Obama's "post-racial" society, this is the kind of leadership we have lacked but so desperately need. I always say this guy should run for president. In the meantime, I guess we'll have to settle for this book—the right book about race for these racially confusing times.

1

From Rebellion to Respect for the Badge

AS THE SQUAD CAR ROLLED PAST our house just outside the projects of Milwaukee one summer afternoon, I clenched my hand into a tight fist. My friends and I had been hanging out in the front yard, and I was in a rebellious mood.

It was 1969. The previous year, it seemed our nation was changing at breakneck speed. Martin Luther King Jr. was shot dead outside his room at the Lorraine Motel in Memphis; Robert Kennedy was murdered in Los Angeles; *Apollo 8* was the first manned spacecraft to orbit the moon; fictional *Star Trek* character *Enterprise* Capt. James Kirk kissed Lt. Nyota Uhura in America's first televised interracial kiss; and riots broke out at the Democratic National Convention in Chicago. Also, two black American athletes made history at the summer Olympics after winning gold and bronze medals in the 200-meter race. As our national anthem played, Tommie Smith and John Carlos stood on the podium, shocking the world with heads bowed and black-gloved fists raised high in the air to protest discrimination against black people back home. As they left the podium, the crowd booed, but Smith didn't back down. "We are black, and we are proud of being black," he said. "Black America will understand what we did tonight."

We did.

Watching those Olympic Games about two thousand miles away in Milwaukee, we knew inherently that there was something wrong with America. The raised fist had become the universal symbol of black solidarity. That's why, when the police car got in front of my house at 39th and Kaul Avenue, I thrust my fist into the air and planted my feet into the ground.

Black pride. Black power. You aren't welcome here, my raised fist conveyed to the police officers.

At least that's what I *wanted* them to understand. The cops apparently didn't get the message. Instead of being intimidated, they suddenly stopped their car. Two officers got out and began walking over to me. The grins on my friends' faces faded. Out of respect, I lowered my arm, walked to the policemen, and looked down at my shoes. But just as the police began to open their mouths to question me, my worst nightmare came true.

The front door of my house creaked behind me and out came my father, David Clarke Sr. He squinted in the afternoon sun as he assessed the situation, and my heart nearly stopped beating.

My Dad, the Ranger

My father joined the US Army when he was sixteen, just three years older than I was when I raised my fist in defiance. He was assigned to a tank battalion in Fort Knox, Kentucky, but he really wanted to be a paratrooper. Ranger training hadn't even been offered to black soldiers before then, but he was able to go to Fort Benning, Georgia, to train with the Second Ranger Infantry Company—the army's first, last, and only all-black Rangers. Since he was the only person in the Rangers to come from a tank battalion, they called him "Tank."

When war broke out in Korea, UN forces pushed the North Korean Army as far north as the Yalu River. But when Chinese troops poured over the border to help the North Koreans, America realized the South Koreans might face defeat if they didn't fully utilize the skills of these black Rangers. Could black Rangers be elite? There were many differing opinions on that, but the army needed them. Consequently, members of the Second Ranger Infantry Company had two very divided lives.

Stateside, they were black soldiers living under the inequity of seg- regation. In combat, however, they were well-respected members of a top-notch fighting force. Though the army was the last military branch to comply with Harry S. Truman's 1948 executive order committing the government to integrating the armed services, the inefficiencies of separate hospitals or aid stations were unaffordable; combat troops of all ethnicities were mixed together. On March 23, 1951, the Second Ranger Infantry Company loaded onto a plane headed to Munsan-ni for a jump. One black Ranger, as he prepared to make history, observed, "It took the Chinese to integrate the American Army."[1]

Buffalo Soldiers. That's what they called them. Though there are a few stories floating around about the origin of the nickname, apparently the Cheyenne saw black soldiers fighting in the plains back in 1870 and compared their curly hair and color to those of buffalos. In World War I, black soldiers adopted the nickname and wore a shoulder patch of a solitary black buffalo to indicate their division. In 1942, they even somehow got a live buffalo as a mascot. By the time my dad was in the army, the term was a sign of respect. Embracing the name helped the soldiers declare, "We are Rangers *and* we carry the tradition of earlier Buffalo soldiers. We are strong, we are resilient, and we are united to destroy the enemy."

But no matter how determined they were, they had no idea what they were getting into. The war was hard on the Second Ranger Infantry Company even before they got into battle. Frostbite was rampant since temperatures in Korea dipped below zero and bitter winds ripped through the combat clothing left over from World War II.

One January morning, they headed out to meet the enemy. My dad was a First Platoon BAR runner. BAR stood for Browning Automatic Rifle. He carried his weapon and ammo for the 60mm mortar over an old, abandoned railroad track. Since they found it too difficult to reload in the mountainous terrain, the Rangers doubled the amount of ammunition they carried.

That evening, they ate C rations and slept on the frozen ground. The next morning, they awakened stiff and cold and began making their way down the treacherous mountain. During their journey, they received enemy fire. One American soldier was shot while eating a can of beans. Within seconds another soldier was killed with several others wounded. My dad, his friend Corporal Lawrence "Poochie" Williams, and the others took cover behind a boulder, but they didn't have a good line of sight to the enemy. "Put some fire on those hills," my dad heard, an order he obeyed. Turns out, the boulder wasn't as protective as they'd hoped, especially when they realized that some fire was coming from behind.

"Sergeant Freeman, Poochie got hit in his head!" my dad heard just as his friend's corpse nearly fell on him. Poochie had hated wearing his steel helmet and wasn't wearing one on that fateful day—it's not clear it would've saved his life. He got hit in the head, and the bullet came out of his eye. A bullet ripped open another Ranger's chin, and another was hit twice and fatally in the neck. Private First Class Robert St. Thomas was near my father when a bullet went through his foot.

"Is that a bullet hole?" he asked as he peeled back his shoe pack. It was so cold he could barely feel the wound.

"You've been hit," my dad confirmed.

By that time, my dad had used all of his ammo but one magazine, and soldiers were getting shot all around him. "Everybody out!" he heard. As they retreated under a shower of enemy fire, many more Americans were killed or wounded. This included St. Thomas. The last time my dad saw him alive was when he was inspecting his bullet-pierced, frozen foot.

"Come on out," a soldier named Dude Walker with an M1 said. "I got you covered."

Because of his own bravery and the bravery of others—but most important by the hand of God—my dad survived that skirmish. But no matter how brave they were, it wasn't enough for some people.

The Second Ranger Infantry Company was attached to the X Corps, led by General Edward M. Almond. He was one of those people in the military who still didn't support racial integration of the troops. "No white man wants to be accused of leaving the battle line. The Negro doesn't care," he said. "People think being from the South we don't like Negroes. Not at all. But we understand his capabilities. And we don't want to sit at the table with them."[2] He frequently discussed black soldiers' incompetence, cowardly nature, and ignorance.

No matter what the general said, the Second Ranger Infantry Company served with valor and courage. They received the Combat Infantry Streamer awarded to units that received more than 65 percent of casualties in a particular engagement.

General Douglas MacArthur recognized the importance and historical significance of Dad's company. "I have one criticism of negro troops who fought under my command in the Korean War," he said. "They didn't send me *enough* of them."

My dad returned to Milwaukee as a sergeant with a chest full of medals. There, he married Geraldine and worked for the post office. Together, they had five kids. I was the second-born but oldest son, and we had a peaceful life. When I was younger, we lived in a housing project on the north side called Berryland, but after I turned twelve, we moved to a compact house with white aluminum siding and wide awnings a few blocks away. My parents lived frugally, living simply so they could send all of their kids to Catholic school. We never had new cars or went on vacations. Well, to be clear, our idea of a vacation was piling in the car and visiting my grandmother in Beloit.

Every morning, we'd get bundled up and walk about five blocks to St. Albert School, a large off-white brick building surrounded by an asphalt playground and a chain-link fence. The nuns at school held complete sway over our behavior, their raised rulers coming down hard on us when we strayed from the straight and narrow path. We knew not to cross them in the classroom, but our fear extended beyond the schoolhouse doors. Blocks away, we felt the lingering effects of their discipline. As soon as we got about three blocks from school, we knew to cross the road and walk double file down the sidewalk until we reached the intersection where the crossing guard would escort us across the street to school. Why double file? That configuration, the nuns told us, allowed two kids to be on the sidewalk without blocking the way for any adult pedestrians who might be coming our way. We never even dreamed of doing something as radical as walking in a group down the sidewalk as if we owned it, making anyone who walked toward us go around us . . . even outside their domain. There at St. Albert, I developed my love of learning and books, but I also loved sports.

My hero was my dad's brother Frank. Named after Franklin Delano Roosevelt, he was a great athlete who was drafted out of the University of Colorado in the fifth round of the 1956 NFL draft by the Cleveland Browns. He played one season in Ohio before the Cowboys picked him up in the expansion draft. For Dallas, he became the first receiver with more than one thousand receiving yards. He's often described as the first black athlete who was a star, even though his host city was racially divided at the time. He held the Cowboys season touchdown reception record until a few years ago when Terrell Owens broke it. Terrell signed a football and sent it to my uncle when that happened. Frequently, people ask me where I got my affinity for my trademark cowboy hat and cowboy boots. It goes back to my love of my uncle and his success for Dallas.

My dad's other brother, Edwin Clarke, wrote for *The Milwaukee Journal* and hosted black public affairs programs on local television. My father had, I suppose, a less prominent job. Every Sunday, he'd get up and meticulously iron his postman's uniform before the start of the week. The man could press a seam. My mother was a stay-at-home mom until we were school age. Then she worked as a secretary for Milwaukee Public Schools. Even though they were working parents, they kept a strict rein on us kids.

My friends would go to a nearby train trestle, grocery store, or corner drugstore after school, but my dad allowed me to go only to our neighborhood park, which was just an empty field a few blocks from home. My father said, "No farther," so the park was the unofficial boundary line of my life. I didn't know how big the city was because I rarely left the neighborhood. My siblings and I weren't out running the streets. My father didn't go for that, nor did he go for hanging out. Everything that I did took place within a few steps of my home. When the streetlights went on at dusk, I'd better be at home. If not, my dad would drive through the streets looking for me. Once I got home, he hid my shoes to ensure I was not tempted to sneak out.

"You have no business standing around doing nothing," he always told me. "You'll be at our house."

"How can I see my friends?"

"If your friends want to see you so bad, they can come over here." He didn't add "where I can keep an eye on you," but he didn't have to. He had the reputation of being the strictest father on the block. He wouldn't tolerate disrespect and definitely didn't suffer fools. I bristled under his watchful eye, but I also knew he had my back.

An Unforgettable Moment

A few months before I raised my fist to the cops, I had been on our neighborhood playground, which was nothing more than an asphalt basketball court (with bases painted on it for baseball too) and a swing set. I was swinging with my buddies, all who were white, when some older kids came up. Back then, teenagers who were sixteen to eighteen were either "hood" or "college" (pronounced *coleej*). These guys were hoods.

"Get off that swing, n—," one of them said to me.

Even though I lived in a predominantly white neighborhood, it was the first time someone had called me that word publicly. I got off the swing and shuffled home, embarrassed and hurt not so much because of the name but because I'd been called it in front of my friends. I'd never seen myself as different, but there it was—the color of my skin pointed out in the most embarrassing fashion.

"What's wrong?" my mom asked when I walked in the house. I was bawling.

"We were on the swings," I cried, "and they kicked us off and one called me n—."

"David, you know what I always say. Sticks and stones will break your bones, but words can never hurt you."

I tried to find comfort in her singsongy advice, but it was cold comfort. That's when my dad came in the room.

"What's going on?" As soon as my mother explained the situation, he started to head out the door.

"Dave, don't," she said. "Stay."

But my dad pointed at me and said, "Come with me."

"Those guys?" my dad asked when we walked into the park. The hoods were still on the swings, slowly going back and forth as they talked. My dad went straight to them and with a raised voice said, "Get off those swings!"

They obeyed more quickly than I had complied to their demand a few minutes earlier.

"Which one of you called my son a n—?" he asked.

"It wasn't me, it wasn't me," they all said. They knew my dad was a no-nonsense man, and they were rightfully afraid of him. He didn't lay a hand on them, but he put the fear of God in them.

My dad stuck up for me, and I knew I would never forget this moment. But he also was adamant that I was not a victim. He never encouraged the racial hypersensitivity seen too frequently today. Though he never talked to me about it outright, I knew he didn't like identity politics and wouldn't have his son participate in such nonsense.

When I raised my fists to the police, as soon as my father appeared in the door, my friends' curiosity over the impending interaction with the police disappeared. They grabbed their bikes and left—no words spoken. Even they respected my father.

"What's going on here?" my dad asked, his eyes squinting as he tried to adjust to the afternoon autumn sun. "Is there a problem, officer?"

"Your son called us over," one said. "We were driving by, and he raised his hand. We figured he needed us."

The other added, "Actually, he raised his *fist*."

I was a rule follower, so a raised fist was not typical behavior. On that day, this usually shy and reserved kid wanted to impress my friends; I wanted the cops to know I didn't like them; I wanted to make a statement. Now that I'm older and fully appreciate all that my dad went through in the war—the segregation, the insults, the slander, the deaths around him—without complaining, I bet he couldn't imagine that his kid had a reason in the world to be angry at those cops.

My dad placed his hand on my shoulder and said—without changing his calm tone of voice—"I'll take care of it."

The officers nodded, got back in their car, and drove away. I would've rather been handcuffed and dragged down to the station than be left there with my dad. When we got inside the house, he turned to me and asked, "What do you think you're doing?"

I didn't answer. I knew not to make excuses.

"You never mess with the police," he said. "Never."

There was something in the tone of his voice and his steady gaze. The police knew my dad would handle my attitude. My dad knew he could handle it. And I knew, beyond a shadow of a doubt, that I would never do that again.

And I didn't.

The Irony of Life

In an ironic twist of fate, I actually became a Milwaukee police officer. For eleven years, I patrolled my beats on foot or in a car going through the streets of our city just like those two officers so many years earlier. In 1989, I was promoted to detective. Nine months later, I was selected for the specialized Homicide Division, where I helped investigate more than four hundred murders over a four-year span. In 1992, I was promoted to lieutenant of detectives and assigned to the Criminal Investigation Bureau as shift commander of the Crimes Against

Property Division, the Violent Crimes Unit. In 1996, I was promoted again to become captain of police and soon became commander of the department's First District (Milwaukee's business and entertainment center) and ultimately the Department's Intelligence Division. And all of that was *before* I became sheriff of Milwaukee County.

Over the years, I've had a front-row seat to the staggering ways our nation has changed, and believe me, a great deal has changed, as life always does, but not always for the better.

Here's how my story would go in 2017:

A black kid and his friends are hanging out on their front yard when they see a patrol car coming slowly through their neighborhood.

One kid curses at the police officers, picks up a rock, and throws it at their car. His friends laugh and extend their middle fingers to the cops. The car stops, and the officers get out.

"You can't come over here, pig," one yells. "This is private property!"

"We're on the sidewalk," the officer says, his hand held up to calm the boys. "This is public property."

The door opens, and the mother of one boy runs down the steps as she shouts, "Get outta here! Why are you bothering these boys?"

The situation escalates as one kid picks up a rock and hits a policeman square in the face.

The other police officer drops the kid, putting him in handcuffs. The mother, wailing all the while, whips out her cell phone as the policeman tries to hold him down *and* keep the others from interfering with the arrest.

"Quit brutalizing him!" she screams. "He's a good kid!"

The kid resists arrest, screaming, "We were just talking!" The dramatic footage leads the six o'clock news. For the next few days, Black Lives Matter protestors set up camp around the boy's house. The officer is accused of racism and is put on leave. The YouTube video of the incident is seen more than a million times, #TalkingWhileBlack becomes a widely used hashtag, and political pundits on both sides of the aisle use this incident as a Rorschach test.

When you watch this, do you see an out-of-control police force or an out-of-control kid? Your answer says a great deal about you. Fights on Facebook break out among the closest of friends, and the fabric of society tears just a little more.

What has happened to America? It seems as though incidents such as these—and others far worse—happen across the nation with startling regularity.

You probably picked up this book because you have seen me on television or heard me on the radio. But I have to admit: most handwringing pundits have no idea what they're talking about when it comes to "police brutality," racial politics, and the intersection of law enforcement and some of the poorer people of America. I want to shed light on these topics—and more—to give Americans a better understanding of the scope of the problem, the challenges we're facing, and—I hope—some solutions.

Scratch that. Thomas Sowell is famous for saying, "There are no solutions, just tradeoffs." I agree. As America becomes increasingly divided and polarized, there are no easy answers to what ails us, but it's never too late to view our problems with open eyes, look to God for answers, stop blaming the wrong people, and realize that what has worked in the past might still work in the future.

2

Political Shakedown:
Give Me Your $29 or Else

IN JANUARY 2002, Milwaukee County Sheriff Leverett F. Baldwin resigned midway through his term, so I decided to apply. Ultimately Republican Governor Scott McCallum would select from the ten people who threw their hat in the ring.

On the application for the appointment, one question gave me pause: "If selected, what party will you run under during the next election?" After being appointed, the replacement would be facing a political campaign in another five months. I wasn't terribly interested in politics.

Republican? Democrat? I placed my pen in the "Republican" box and checked it. I wasn't incredibly wedded to that designation, but it felt like a better fit than the Democratic Party. I was a "law and order" police officer, of course, which seemed more naturally attuned to the GOP. The next portion was an interview with a panel of six people, which I felt I'd handled pretty well. The only thing to do was wait. But there was one slight problem. Every year, I go on vacation with my wife, Julie, her sister, and her husband to celebrate our anniversary, and I worried I'd miss the call.

"I just wanted you to know I'm going out of the country," I told the governor's chief legal counsel. "So I wanted to leave you the number of the condo where we'll be staying."

I remember sitting poolside in the Cayman Islands when my brother-in-law called down, "Hey, David, the governor's office is on the phone."

"You're lying!" I yelled up to him.

"No, it's the governor's office," he said more urgently, his hand covering the phone receiver.

Reluctantly, I went up there and grabbed the phone. He wasn't lying.

The first thing the governor's representative said was, "Don't read anything into this, but if you get the appointment, you need to consider running as a Democrat."

He had barely finished the sentence before I blurted, "Absolutely not!"

"This is a Democratic county," he said. "You can't get elected as a Republican here."

"Sure I can," I explained. "I have a good message, and I know a thing or two about police work." But I was naïve because I thought you could win an elected office based on principles alone. Though I'd lived in Milwaukee my whole life, I wasn't involved in elected politics and had no idea what I was getting into.

"Look, if you get the appointment and have to run in the election," he said, "you'll need to be a Democrat."

Still, I wasn't happy.

"Just sleep on it," he said. "Enjoy the rest of your vacation. We think you'll be busy when you get back."

That's when I realized I'd probably get the appointment.

But me a Democrat?

The Rumor Mill

After we returned home, Julie and I met with Governor McCallum. I imagined the first topic of discussion would be my choice of a political party, so I was quite shocked when he said, "I have to ask a delicate question. Why does the Milwaukee Police union hate you?"

At the time, I was no longer in the union, even though I'd been in it fourteen years. I didn't know what to say.

"I was told appointing you would be my biggest political mistake."

Apparently, the union had been calling the governor's office and encouraging him to choose a different replacement.

After a brief pause, he said, "Also, I have to ask, are you telling us absolutely *everything*?" He looked back and forth between us.

The governor was facing a reelection campaign in five months as well, so I understood his need to know exactly who he was dealing with. But I sensed he was fishing for something. "What are you talking about? I've been completely transparent."

"We're hearing something about a domestic violence incident."

My blood ran cold. The same rumor had emerged when I was a captain in District One—the downtown district. One day when I had gone into work, my lieutenant entered my office and said, "I heard the police came to your house last night to investigate domestic violence."

"What?" I had asked, incredulous. "There weren't police at my house last night."

A few more cops had approached me about it over the course of the next few days, and friends had also begun calling Julie.

"He doesn't beat me," she had told them, exasperated. The rumor had even reached her parents in northern Wisconsin, putting her in an awkward position. "No, everything's fine," she had reassured them.

At the time, I had gone to the office of the assistant chief, who would've been notified if one of his captains had been called for domestic violence.

"Hey, you guys have to help me kill this rumor," I had told him. "It's not true."

"I know," he had said, "but after consulting with the chief, he thinks it would add fuel to the fire if we put out an official statement. Just let it go."

"I want my name cleared," I had protested before ultimately submitting to their counsel.

I regretted that decision now as I was looking into the eyes of a very concerned governor.

"It's a hoax," I said immediately. "It's not like a call was made and the cops said there was a misunderstanding. There was no call . . . ever."

"Julie," the governor asked, "what can you tell me about it?"

She began to cry. "I've never called the police," she explained. "No police have ever been to my house about domestic violence. Ever."

The media had poked around for gossip but found nothing. That's when the rumor morphed. It hadn't happened in Milwaukee, the new rumor suggested, but in northern Wisconsin. That had caused the media to call Green Bay's police department looking for something—anything—that would have given them dirt on me. When nothing turned up, the rumor changed to suggest the chief had ordered the destruction of all the records of my domestic violence call.

Have you ever heard of the logical fallacy of a loaded question? The most classic example is this: "Have you stopped beating your wife?" Whether the person answers yes or no, he's in a bad spot. Either answer presupposes that he has, in fact, beaten his wife at some time in the past.

I felt as if I was in that horrible position. How do you deny something that never happened? All you can do is go into denial mode, which makes you look guilty. The fact that you can't be proven innocent leaves a shadow of uncertainty. Other than the fact that there were no records and Julie backed me up, I couldn't prove it didn't happen.

To make matters worse, I wasn't sure who I'd offended. I had been an up-and-comer, so I have to assume the rumors had started because people knew I was going places. Perhaps some had believed I'd gotten the promotion they deserved. I finished number two on the lieutenant's list, and although I had been slightly disappointed not to have received the top score, I knew I had done my best to prepare myself, using vacation time and every spare minute off duty to study. The only other time I had worked harder in my life was when I was finishing my bachelor's and master's degrees. But when the scores came out, immediately people claimed the test was fixed for minorities. I tried not to let it get to me, but it did.

Maybe the rumors were started because people thought I didn't deserve what I was getting. Maybe it was because I was married to a nice-looking white woman. Who knows? I just knew someone had attempted to assassinate my character, and it had followed me for years.

After the governor talked to Julie, he turned to me and said, "The fact that the Milwaukee Police Association was working against you helps you. I'm mad they treated you that way."

At the news conference announcing my appointment, I proudly stood before my parents, Julie's parents, my colleagues, and my friends. Yes, it had been a tough road, but I had survived the slander, and my merit was obvious to all.

Guess the first question out of a reporter's mouth.

"Do you want to talk about this domestic violence accusation?"

I was stunned. Talk about someone raining on your parade. I

looked at Julie and hoped she wouldn't start crying. "No, that's just a rumor," I said, trying not to show my irritation. "It's not true."

Later, I talked to the reporter, who said her outlet had forced her to ask the question even though she knew it wasn't true. I wish she'd had the integrity to resign instead of sully my reputation.

Many times, pundits in the media complain there are no good candidates for political office. But as soon as decent people put themselves out there to do something good, the pundits immediately attack them with lies and slander. It's no wonder "good people" don't want to put themselves through that kind of scrutiny and unfair treatment.

The next question from a reporter was, "So you'll be running as a Republican?"

"No," I said. "I'll be running as a Democrat."

Gasps were heard across the room. Some people applauded.

Remember, I had no political experience, and this seemingly rogue announcement made it look as though I was more liberal than I was. Though the governor's office knew of my plans in advance—and, in fact, had been forced to convince me to run as a Democrat—I was suddenly a prominent Democrat in the city of Milwaukee. That was fine by me since I was up for election very shortly.

A Cover Charge for This Party

I attended my first Democratic fund-raiser, hoping that the Democratic Party would show me the ropes. I hoped to meet people from the party and get a feel for their beliefs. That's not what happened.

While I was there, a woman walked up to me and shoved a 3 x 5 card in my face. "Fill this in," she demanded. "And send in your twenty-nine dollars."

"What is it?"

"You have to join the party," she said, barely looking at me. "You're running as a Democrat, so you have to join the party."

"You have to tell me a little something about what I'm joining," I said. I knew they had already endorsed my opponent—the hand-picked successor of the previous sheriff—so I wondered about the upside.

"It doesn't matter," she said. "You're running as a Democrat."

I knew right then and there that I wouldn't join this party if it saved my life. I don't need a party that presumes my allegiance without going to any trouble to court me or convince me. That's where black Americans are right now in 2017 too. Blacks have been taken for granted far too long by the Democratic Party, and Republicans have historically failed to reach out to us effectively. We're in a difficult position both ways, and it's hard to break through society's preconceived notions.

So as a political novice in a party hostile to me from the get-go, I reached out to Democratic fund-raiser Barb Candy, who told me she'd only help me in my reelection campaign if I got Bill Christofferson, the media maven who was also running Governor Jim Doyle's campaign, to sign on as my strategist.

"I don't know him," I said.

"He's the most cutthroat strategist in Wisconsin," she said, sliding me a piece of paper. "And you need him on your side. Here's his number."

That was Mother's Day, and I had no campaign manager even though the election was in November. Time was running out.

"I've never run a sheriff's campaign," Bill said when I called him. "Plus, I don't know anything about you. What does a sheriff even run on?"

"Law and order," I said. "What else?"

Bill was a huge leftist liberal, and I was an unknown commodity. However, he somehow decided I was worth the effort even though a kerfuffle emerged about my refusal to join the Democratic Party.

"Bill," I explained, "the lady stuck a 3 x 5 card in my face. They'd endorsed my opponent! I didn't want them to presume I'd join them just because they wanted me to."

"Look, if you join, the newspaper will stop writing articles about it," he said. "It'll effectively take the issue off the table." I kept listening. "If you don't join, though, I don't think it'll make a difference."

That settled it for me. I'd run as a Democrat, but I wouldn't join the party. Bill, a strategy genius, told me that to win an election, we had to have the right candidate, a good message, and enough money. In that first campaign, thanks to Bill, we had all three. Well, I guess I can take credit for the "candidate" part. I was forty-five years old—more energetic than I am now—and people seemed to like me. Since I'm a natural recluse when not wearing my badge, Julie was shocked that I did so well campaigning.

"It was almost hard to explain," Bill later reflected. "He was kind of a natural . . . He's a fresh face, somebody who says what's on his mind."[1]

Barb signed on as my political fund-raiser. "David has a clearer sense of who he is than just about anybody I've worked for in twenty-some years," she said.

Together, Barb and Bill advised me to make the news once a week to raise my name identification in Milwaukee, but I ended up in the paper nearly every day. Consequently, we raised more than $165,000—a record amount of money for the sheriff's race (the previous sheriff had raised $45,000). I won my first election and was elated.

Later, I met with Bill to discuss a possible mayoral campaign. He said, "I can't help you run if you won't help me elect other Democrats once you're elected."

"Well, you're right about that," I said. "I can't help you do that."

"I can't work for somebody who's for George Bush," he said. And so, we parted ways.

To this day, Bill regrets helping me. "The biggest mistake I ever made in politics is helping Clarke get elected," he said on an urban radio station.

And he was right, I suppose.

When I won my first campaign, I knew I couldn't have done it without his help. He was such a brilliant strategist, but I didn't need him beside me every step of my political life because I learned so much from that first campaign that I was able to use his strategies in my next three races.

Outspent but Not Overmatched

With my newfound prominence in the city, R. J. Johnson—the equivalent of Bill on the conservative side—had reached out to me to help Scott Walker get elected. He asked me to sign a fund-raising letter on behalf of Walker, which I was happy to do. I'd tried to stay away from the Republican Party, but I knew Walker needed a boost. I was sure that the press would run me over the coals, and they did.

Of course, headlines emerged, "Clarke Helps Republican Scott Walker." I knew helping Walker was the right thing to do although it would cause me political trouble. There comes a time when you have to stiffen your back and sign your name to help people who are the good guys.

As you can imagine, the Democrats quickly got sick of me, so they decided to do what Democrats do best—undercut the only black sheriff in the state of Wisconsin.

"He's not a real Democrat," they said at first. That didn't work.

"He's not one of us," they said. That didn't stick.

In my fourth campaign, they came up with a more stinging criticism. *Clarke's crazy*, they said. *He's pro-gun, and he's really a Republican.*

I began to worry about that one. Especially since they were able to raise a massive amount of dark money—money that wasn't reportable, money we didn't know they had. Michael Bloomberg's anti-gun PAC wrote a check for just over $150,000[2] to a 501(c)(4) political organization called the Greater Wisconsin Committee (which ironically was started by Bill Christofferson many years ago to raise money to attack conservatives). The Milwaukee County Executive trust fund baby wrote a check for $263,000. At the end of the day, they raised about $800,000 in the effort to defeat me.

I had only $165,000. That was a pretty good amount, since this was not a congressional race or a mayoral contest. We knew the media was giving my opponent a lot of free air time to defeat me, but we had no idea that we were going to be outspent by such a wide margin. Because this money wasn't reportable under campaign finance laws, we weren't prepared for the onslaught of television ads that would frame me as "crazy."

I reached out to Walker's people to ask him to help me. I was shocked when he told me that he wasn't going to be able to publicly help.

"Why won't Walker help me?" I asked R. J. "I got my butt kicked over helping him."

"Well, he doesn't want news articles indicating that he's not a true conservative by helping a Democrat get elected."

It was a hard lesson in politics. Partisanship trumps principle. I still like Walker today. We're friends. I understand that you have to be politically smart, but I wish he'd been less focused on his future in politics and more focused on doing the right thing.

By the time the Left was finished peppering me with negative television ads, I was no longer a political novice. I did great in the black community, I was solid in the suburbs, and in all four campaigns my voters stuck by my side no matter how much dark money came against me.

You know the story of David and Goliath in the Bible?

I guess I'm not named David for nothing.

I have won my primary elections with more than 50 percent of the vote each time.

I've also faced opponents in all of my general elections (in 2014 it was a socialist party candidate), but I won—and won big each time—and I'm here on the national stage to stay.

3

I'm Color-Blind
When It Comes to Crime
and Punishment

"CAN I TAKE THIS ONE for a test drive?" a twenty-four-year-old wearing a dark fleece jacket asked as he approached the used-car salesman. The young man, Lamar Nash, was interested in a silver Tahoe that Wednesday afternoon, and the salesman was eager to move vehicles after the new year. After retrieving the keys from the main office, he tossed them to Nash. But when the salesman walked around to the passenger side to accompany him on his test drive, he heard the unmistakable sound of the doors locking. He tried to open the doors, but the passenger door didn't budge. Sealed shut. Just as he realized that his "customer" was not really interested in test-driving the SUV, Nash slammed on the gas pedal and sped out of the lot.

At 4:25, the call from Andrew Chevrolet came into the police station. Glendale police almost immediately spotted the vehicle on area streets and started pursuing it. My office was notified of the pursuit when Nash drove the stolen SUV onto Interstate 43, because the Milwaukee Sheriff's Department patrols freeways as part of its essential law enforcement services.

One of my deputies on the interstate pulled over into the emergency lane when she heard the call. Soon enough, she saw a silver SUV coming up in lane 2. Behind the Tahoe was a black-and-white squad car that she believed to be the initiating police.

"Should I stop this vehicle?" she radioed.

"We're taking a trailing position" came the response from the Glendale police. High-speed chases are incredibly dangerous, one of the riskiest activities for an officer. The North Shore police had canceled the pursuit because of the heavy traffic that afternoon. "We're *not* requesting that you stop him."

My deputy, who was dressed in full duty uniform, was driving a marked police car but hadn't turned on her lights or sirens. Neither did the black-and-white police car trailing the suspect. My deputy switched from lane 2 to lane 3 to allow the suspect vehicle to pass her. Instead of passing, however, Nash suddenly swerved from his lane into her lane in an attempt to hit her squad car. She darted into the emergency lane to avoid being struck.

"He tried to ram me," she said into the radio.

The police didn't want to chase him at high speed, but they couldn't ignore his maneuver indicating he was violent and dangerous. A high-speed chase began.

The speed limit was fifty-five miles per hour, and he sped away with my deputy in pursuit, now with the squad car's lights and sirens on. By the time Nash approached South Sixth Street, he was driving seventy-nine miles per hour in the emergency lane. Without warning, he braked. My deputy swerved back into the first lane to avoid a rear-end collision, but then Nash deliberately swerved into her lane to try to hit her car. He sped up to ninety, then slowed down to fifty-five. Faster and slower. Left and right. I don't know specifically who was on the road that afternoon, but undoubtedly there were men and women coming home from work, moms and dads carpooling children, young drivers on the interstate for their first time, and older drivers who might not have the reflexes they once enjoyed. All, unknowingly, possible victims.

Then the situation became more complicated. "It looks like the suspect might have a shotgun," she advised the dispatcher on her radio. Though she couldn't see the object he was holding, it looked as though he was racking rounds into a gun. The deputy began to worry about the commuters on the road as she noticed items flying out of the suspect's driver's-side window. It looked like wads of paper—money—and compact discs in hard cases. Other officers in pursuit reported that compact discs had hit their windshields.

Some drivers, no doubt after seeing all of the emergency vehicles in their rearview mirrors, pulled over into the right-hand emergency lane. At one point, Nash swerved into the distress lane to hit the car of a citizen who'd tried to get out of the way. The driver realized what was happening and managed to move far enough over to avoid a collision. Nash then immediately swerved left in an attempt to hit another civilian vehicle in the second lane. That driver swerved into the first lane and avoided being hit.

"Dispatch," my deputy said into her radio, "the suspect vehicle has attempted to ram two civilian vehicles. And I believe," she squinted to make sure she was seeing the scene correctly, "I believe he's taking his shirt off." Driving at a high rate of speed on a packed freeway while the police are chasing you is one thing. Doing all of this while disrobing? That's even more dangerous. The situation was spiraling out of control.

"This is Squad 453 requesting permission to terminate the pursuit," my deputies heard another say over the radio. "Terminate the pursuit" sounded so clean and easy, but this intervention, known as a PIT, short for precision immobilization technique, requires the deputy's squad car to strike the side rear of the suspect's auto. Here's how it works: the deputy aligns his front bumper behind the suspect's back wheel well. Once he gets in that position—mind you, going at a high rate of speed—the deputy steers his squad car right into the fleeing vehicle. If it is done perfectly, the suspect's car is sent into a spin. Most of the time, the fleeing car will stall, which gives the backup police time to surround the suspect. In the best-case scenario, neither the officer nor the suspect is harmed. However, by law, this maneuver is considered to be deadly force because at such a high speed, the fleeing driver could be seriously injured or killed.

There was a long pause on the radio after the officer's request, then a one-word response from the sergeant: "Affirmative."

The rest of the squad cars backed off, allowing this deputy to become the primary pursuit vehicle. That gave the officer enough space to perform the maneuver in a section of the freeway where traffic volume had lessened. Squads from other jurisdictions cleared the area by closing ramps to prevent additional cars from entering the freeway.

At 4:43, it was time to stop this chase. The deputy lined up his vehicle with the Tahoe and veered into it—T-boning it. Both vehicles lurched to the left, hitting a retaining wall. The squad car spun, rolled onto the driver's side, and then landed with its rear in the left emergency lane. The suspect's vehicle bounced off the median, continued westbound in the southbound lanes, and struck the retaining wall in a head-on collision.

As the January evening grew dark, my deputies parked their squad cars and advanced toward him in their trained tactical approach for a felony stop: weapons drawn.

"Show me your hands!" a deputy shouted as he approached the suspect. "Show me your hands!" Dark smoke poured from the Tahoe, obscuring the officer's view of Nash. The officer heard someone racking a shotgun, which caused the officer to yell again, "Show me your hands!"

He moved to get a better view of the suspect, who by that time was out of the vehicle. When Nash finally came into view, the deputy saw that his hands were open and empty.

"Lie on the ground," he shouted. "Don't move or I'll shoot!"

Nash got facedown on the interstate, next to the driver's side of the stolen vehicle. One deputy—who happened to have experience in Expressway Patrol Operations on the SWAT team, with the Detective Bureau, and as an undercover officer in narcotics—pressed his foot on Nash's neck while waiting for the others to arrive to handcuff him. "Get down on the ground!" he yelled, but Nash continued to struggle. When the other officers arrived, he holstered his weapon and assisted in securing the suspect's left arm.

"Stop resisting!" a deputy shouted as Nash continued to struggle to get up. An officer grabbed him by the belt loop and pulled him up, forcing him against a concrete barrier and then the stolen vehicle. "Stop resisting!" he yelled again while Nash pushed and pulled his arms away from the deputies. "Stop resisting," as he tried to get Nash to spread his legs. Without warning, Nash kicked back at the deputy, striking him in the leg.

Finally, they got him into the squad car, where Nash flailed so violently that he kicked out the back window, glass shattering everywhere.

"Yeah, I kicked out your window," he said before getting a faceful of oleoresin capsicum spray—pepper spray.

While the officers were struggling to get Nash under control, the officer who had performed the PIT technique climbed out of his car, shotgun in hand. The vehicle was still lodged on its side, so he hadn't wanted to crawl out of the passenger's-side window only to be attacked by the suspect. He had abrasions on his arm, and his face was bleeding. Otherwise, he looked fine.

They'd done it. The chase covered 17.1 miles, and no one was seriously hurt. When they finally got Nash to the hospital, he was so uncooperative that the nurses had to sedate him three times. Thankfully, Nash suffered only minor injuries, and the doctor released him.

Of course, the incident wasn't really over. A news helicopter from Milwaukee's WTMJ-TV had been following the chase and broadcasting it live to all of Milwaukee.

And, by the way, the suspect was black.

Giving the Police Brutality Myth the "Boot"

I was sitting in my office, looking at a stack of papers that needed signatures.

"Sheriff," one of my inspectors said as he poked his head in the door, "some deputies are involved in a pursuit of a stolen SUV."

"What else?" I asked, sensing he had more to say when he lingered at the door.

"It's being broadcast live by local TV."

The television that hangs in the upper corner of my office is usually tuned to a news station, so I can keep up with what's going on in the world. I turned my leather chair around, flipped the television to the local station, and saw the footage of the high-speed chase unfolding right before my eyes.

Before I turned up the volume on the police radio so I could follow the action there, I stopped to say a prayer. At that time, late afternoon commuter traffic would be heavy. I didn't want some motorist getting hurt or worse. About a person a day is killed because people try to out-run the police.[1] Many of those deaths are just innocent bystanders, and I didn't want that to happen on my watch.

My inspectors sat in the two chairs in front of my desk. They were talking about what they were seeing on screen, but I didn't join in the conversation. As I watched that pursuit unfold, I got real quiet, silent. I think better when I keep my mouth shut. As the images flickered across the screen, I was processing different scenarios: What if we kill an uninvolved motorist? What if one of my deputies gets killed? What do I say to the media? When? I'm responsible if this thing goes bad. Is it smart for me to stay out of it?

The easy thing for me to do was to take high-risk decision making out of my deputies' hands, but that's the cowardly way out. Deciding when, or if, to end this kind of chase is usually made in circumstances full of anxiety and adrenaline, but my people have good field discipline. I expect them to rely on their pursuit driver training, the law with regard to the safety of others, and their own sound judgment. The officers had a street supervisor who was closely monitoring the speed of the pursuit, weather conditions, and traffic volume. I was proud of my law enforcement officers who were choosing to put themselves in harm's way to protect the public.

As for the fleeing suspect? I wasn't too worried about him. He made his bed. He could sleep in it.

The pursuit was lasting longer than I like. Half of all crashes occur in the first two minutes of a police pursuit. More than 70 percent of all collisions happen before the pursuit has gone on seven minutes.[2] By 4:43 p.m., the pursuit had been going on for eighteen minutes, and the probability of death or severe bodily injury was skyrocketing with every additional erratic action. But I had to exercise restraint. I trusted my officers. I wouldn't get involved because I wasn't there. Just listening to the radio and watching TV do not provide enough information to make decisions in the moment.

As I heard the primary pursuit vehicle given permission to perform the requested PIT maneuver, I took a deep breath and said, "God, help us."

On the screen, I watched as the deputy's vehicle struck the suspect's car. I didn't realize it, but I'd been holding my breath.

I, along with much of Milwaukee, watched as the suspect got out of the car and was ordered to lie on the ground. *I bet ratings for this station will be high tonight*, I thought.

When the deputy moved in and used his foot to pin the suspect down, resting his foot on the suspect's neck to keep him from attacking or going for one of the deputies' weapons. His foot rested on the suspect's neck, I thought, *That isn't going to go over well.*

This incident took place years before the #BlackLivesMatter crowd started harassing the police, but black activists have always been eager to side with the criminal and call out the police for any perceived misstep. Even back in 2003. Black activists always cry, "Police brutality!" no matter what the circumstances, no matter how many people's lives are put at risk during whatever criminal activity draws the attention of the police in the first place. In recent years, hashtags like #DrivingWhileBlack, #AmeriKKKa, #ICantBreathe, #EndPoliceBrutality, and #WalkingWhileBlack have popped up on social media to protest what activists believe is the rampant, systematic abuse of black people. This protest-by-hashtag began in 2013, after a mostly white jury acquitted George Zimmerman of all charges in connection with the shooting death of unarmed black teen Trayvon Martin. I want to remind you that "unarmed" does not mean "not dangerous" under the reasonable officer rule of law standard. (I'll talk more about that in a later chapter.)

Much of America was disappointed and confused by the Zimmerman ruling, including Alicia Garza, who was sitting in a California bar when the news broke.[3] She quickly wrote a letter to black people, urging them to act, to organize, and to realize that black lives matter. Her friend Patrisse Cullors was in Los Angeles when she read Garza's post. Cullors commented under the post, creating a hashtag #BlackLivesMatter.

For those of you who have better things to do than follow social media closely, here's how that works. When people want to draw attention to what they're saying on a social media site like Twitter or Facebook, they sometimes put the # symbol before their relevant keyword or phrase (without any spaces) so that it shows up more easily in a search. Also, others can click on a hashtagged word to see other people's tweets on the same subject. When Garza and Cullors—and another friend named Opal Tometi—promoted #BlackLivesMatter on social media, it caught fire.

The *New York Times* called it "the 21st century's first civil rights movement,"[4] while others have claimed it's the most potent racial slogan since "black power."[5] The slogan jumped from phone screens to T-shirts to signs to even an episode of *Law & Order: SVU*.[6] Suddenly, it was more than a hashtag; it was a movement in the form of a political construct popping up when other incidents of racial strife occurred: Michael Brown, Oscar Grant, and Eric Garner. It was an easy and succinct way to encapsulate the frustration people feel about police, and it perpetuated a certain narrative: police are killing black

Americans simply because of their skin color. (Never mind that there is no data or research to support such a claim.)

"To hear the media tell it, America is in the grip of an unprecedented crime wave, an orgy of wanton murder in which heavily armed thugs randomly gun down innocent unarmed people, some of them teens, just for sport," wrote Michael Walsh in the *New York Post*.[7] "Except that these homicidal goons are wearing the blues and badges of American police departments."

Turns out, that is a terrible lie.

It's so misguided that I have dropped a letter when referring to the movement. Black LIES Matter seems to be more accurate. I've been in law enforcement for decades, and I've seen firsthand the care that officers, even white officers, expend—at risk to their own lives—to keep poor minority communities safe. They go about their daily duty, better trained, more educated, and more professional than at any time in our history.

I caused a stir when I appeared on *Fox & Friends* to discuss this phenomenon. The Black LIES Matter crowd was protesting in Manhattan right after a black police officer was murdered in cold blood. This, even though the main group of people in this nation who really believe black lives matter are the men in blue who put on the uniform and go into the inner cities, trying to prevent people from killing each other. When we see the black-on-black crime that happens every single day across America, there's not one single sound of protest from the Black LIES Matter crowd. They're too busy sitting in coffee shops, drinking their lattes, and being snarky on social media to demand change in behavior from the criminals targeting other members of the black community. When I was in the studio and saw the footage of the protestors calling the police horrible names and screaming at them, I have to be honest, it made my blood boil.

"First of all, there is no police brutality in America," I said. I could almost hear the liberals in America collectively gasping. By that, I didn't mean that specific incidents never happen across the country. Brutality is defined as savage physical violence. That might describe foreign terrorists or even Planned Parenthood harvesting baby parts to sell to the highest bidder, but not American policing. I meant that police brutality is no longer systemic, nor is it condoned within our ranks; it is episodic, and we self-correct when we learn about it. "Show me the data, show me the research that demonstrates and supports the lie that law enforcement officers use an inordinate amount of force against black people," I went on to say. "Black people use an inordinate amount of force against themselves and each other in the American ghetto. It is not true about the American police officer, and I'm not going to let anyone come on TV and advocate that."

Here's a Novel Idea—Look at Actual Numbers

Guess what? Now a major newspaper is backing me up. In response to the Black LIES Matter allegations, the *Washington Post* did something no one else had ever attempted: reporters recorded every fatal police shooting in 2015 that occurred in America. What did they find in their year-long study? Less than 4 percent of fatal police shootings were of unarmed black people. Here's the money quote: "The great majority of people who died at the hands of the police fit at least one of three categories: they were wielding weapons, they were suicidal or mentally troubled, or they ran when officers told them to halt."[8] Also, in 75 percent of these fatal shootings, "police were under attack or defending someone who was." This caused *National Review* to conclude, "The chances of an innocent black man being gunned down by racist cops are vanishingly small."[9]

Michael Walsh writing in a *New York Post* article put it succinctly:

"You have a better chance of being killed in a violent storm (1 in 68,000) or slipping in the tub (1 in 11,500) than being shot by a cop, no matter what color you are."[10]

In other words, Black LIES Matter and its predecessor, the National Association for the Advancement of Colored People (NAACP), have taught black people that they can't trust the police, that their futures are hopeless, and that American institutions are against them. But that's only because they want to separate all actions from their consequences.

Supreme Court Justice Clarence Thomas was once asked if there were any areas in which the civil rights establishment, including the NAACP, was doing good work. This was his response:

No. I can't think of any . . . There were grand opportunities for them to focus on the proper education of minority kids, the kids who are getting the worst education, and instead they're talking about integration. . . . I went to segregated schools. You can really learn how to read off those books, even if white folks aren't there. I think segregation is bad, I think it's wrong, it's immoral. I'd fight against it with every breath in my body, but you don't need to sit next to a white person to learn how to read and write. The NAACP needs to say that.

But then he got to the heart of the issue:

You've got a situation recently where the president of the NAACP or one of his spokespersons is defending a kid who punched out a teacher, Give me a break! How . . . are the kids going to learn if they can punch out the teacher? I would have died if I'd done something like that and I went back home to my grandfather—literally died. You've got to have some standards of morality, some strong positive statements about expectations—and those organizations could do that. Instead, they spend their time telling minority kids that it is hopeless out here. Why is it hopeless? Because Ronald Reagan is making it hopeless. When Ronald Reagan is gone, why are you going to tell them that it's hopeless? Because the government isn't spending enough money. It will always be hopeless if that's the reason. You don't have any control over that. What you do have control over is yourself. They should be telling these kids that freedom carries not only benefits, it carries responsibilities. You want to be free, you want to leave your parents' house? Then you've got to earn your own living, you've got to pay your own mortgage, pay your own rent, buy your own car, and pay for your own food. You've got to learn how to take care of yourself, learn how to raise your kids, how to go to school and prepare for a job and take risks like everybody else.[11]

That was during the 1980s. Since then, the so-called civil rights groups have gone even farther off the rails trying to insulate people from terrible behavior, laziness, insubordination, and resentment. The bottom line is this: If you stop when a cop tells you to stop, and you don't point a gun at a cop or try to fight him or her, you'll probably survive your encounter with the police.

But that's not the message the black activists want to convey. No matter how wrong, misguided, reckless, and dangerous a black person might be acting, they'll side with that person over the police every time. That's why I knew, as soon as I saw on television my officer place his boot on Lamar Nash's neck, that I'd be hearing from them soon enough.

I was right.

Within days, the complaint came. It was from an official of the city of Racine's local chapter of the NAACP saying the officer who placed his foot on the suspect's neck used—you guessed it—excessive force. I ordered an internal investigation, something that I do on all citizen complaints, to look more closely at the incident.

In the meantime, the NAACP president, Beverly Hicks, went to the press. "When [the suspect] was on the ground, he wasn't resisting," she said to the *Journal Times*. "I didn't see the need for officers to react the way they did . . . I guess the guy was wrong, but he's still a human being and [the sheriff's deputies] still need to look at their actions."[12] Note that she couldn't bring herself to say definitively that Nash was "wrong"— even after stealing a vehicle, trying to ram innocent civilians and police officers off the road, and breaking out the window of a squad car.

But the NAACP wasn't familiar with me. Newly elected, I was an unknown entity. After all, I am a black Democrat in Milwaukee. I think the black racialists (people who view everything through the prism of race) thought they had "one of their own" as the new sheriff of Milwaukee County. They saw my skin. They figured I'd be on their side.

They would soon be disabused of this notion.

About a week after the incident, I held a news conference in the Sheriff's Office Operations Center. I walked the attendees through the video of the incident and informed them that my internal investigation concluded that the officer's use of force was reasonable under the circumstances. Once and for all, I wanted to settle the issue, to stop the allegations, and to clear the names of the brave deputies.

A week later some black community agitators organized a community forum for a discussion of my decision. As the room filled with about fifty concerned citizens, NAACP representatives, and the local television media, I thought, *Here we go!*

The meeting was called to order. I immediately showed the footage from the news helicopter, offering my observations as the film rolled. When the moment came in the video of the deputy putting his boot on the suspect's neck, I paused it.

"I talked to the deputy, who explained why he used this tactic," I said. I always believe addressing issues head-on is best. "He wanted to make sure the guy would not get up from the ground, something that has happened before in these situations." The faces of the people in the crowd remained hard, frozen in incredulity. "He feared he might end up fighting for his weapon, and—to be honest—that was my thought as I watched it on television just like you did." A few people talked to each other, obviously unmoved by the explanation. "But I'm here to tell you that I've ruled that the officer's tactic was reasonable under the circumstances."

The talking grew louder as people began to shuffle in their seats and call out questions.

"Do you teach your officers to place their foot on people's necks even after they're on the ground?" someone piped up from the back of the room.

"We don't teach it," I said, "But it seemed to work pretty well, didn't it? We can see from the videotape that it's not time for milk and cookies, nor was it time to exchange pleasantries."

Obviously my decision did not sit well with the race hustlers. I didn't care. It was the right decision under the circumstances. This was one of the early glimpses for the public that I was not going to put up with nonsense. But I wasn't finished yet.

"I took you through the entire incident because I wanted to point out the danger the suspect placed *everybody* in," I said. "But it seems you still believe this is a race issue, right?"

People nodded, and I heard someone sarcastically say, "Yes, sir."

"Let me see a show of hands," I said. "I want to see how many think this is about race?" Every hand went up. "So, it's unanimous," I said. Then, I held up an 8 x 10 picture of the deputy—the *black* deputy. "This is the officer who used his boot."

The room fell silent as everyone was absolutely gobsmacked. The helicopter footage, which was shot in the dark, wasn't clear enough to show the race of the officer. The media coverage had described the officer as Caucasian. Everyone assumed that this was yet another incident of a white cop using excessive force with a black kid. "He wasn't white," I said. "And it wasn't excessive."

Everyone started murmuring. They'd been had. They'd jumped to a conclusion without waiting for the facts from the moment the incident happened.

"Hey," someone yelled from the back of the room. "Black officers can be racist too!"

Typical rationalization to save face.

"Okay, then I'll ask the question again," I said. "How many people believe this man is a racist?" No hands went up.

The people in that room were not pleased with me, but we'd come to an uneasy truce. Truth be told, I got many compliments from people in the black community who rightly called the suspect's behavior outrageous. They are a silent majority for fear of being ostracized by other blacks. But on that night, the shallowness of the activists had been exposed, and they knew I wasn't going to let them get away with their war on police.

Not on my watch.

4

Guess What? Prison Is Supposed to Be Unpleasant

"YOU HAVE *GOT* TO BE KIDDING ME," I said, holding papers I'd just been served. "I'm getting sued?"

My secretary, walking by for coffee, paused at my door.

"By whom?"

"Terrance Prude," I read.

"Should that name ring a bell?" she asked.

I read down the complaint and smiled in disbelief. "He's an *inmate*."

In 2007, then County Executive Scott Walker decided to move the Milwaukee House of Correction from the county executive's authority to the sheriff's office for oversight. Things at the jail weren't good. To figure out just how bad they'd gotten, California-based corrections expert Dr. Jeffrey A. Schwartz documented dozens of organizational, administrative, and operational problems. He said ours was one of the most poorly run detention facilities he had seen in decades of inspecting lockup facilities: It had a $5 million deficit and was plagued with a lack of discipline, poor supervision, employee sick use abuse, inmate fights, and excessive and unnecessary overtime use. More than four hundred inmates had escaped their electronic monitoring.[1]

"These problems will take at least five years to change," said Dr. Schwartz, but he definitely didn't know me. I inherited 1,100 inmates being held in deplorable conditions. I wasn't going to drag my heels when people's lives were at stake. Neither was I going to whine about the horrible situation I'd been handed. Instead, I rolled up my sleeves, put an organizational change team in place, and went to work.

Over the next year, I wiped out the deficit; inmate fights became rare; employee attendance improved; overtime was within budget. Also every inmate who had escaped electronic monitoring had been located and arrested by an absconder unit I created. The facility became a well-functioning part of county government.

When Dr. Schwartz did another evaluation, he was certainly surprised, and his report showed it:

Sheriff David A. Clarke Jr. assumed responsibility for the deeply troubled Milwaukee HoC on January 1, 2009. The positive and comprehensive transformation of that facility in less than a year's time is nothing short of miraculous. That is not hyperbole but is the carefully considered conclusion of the author based on over thirty years of observing and studying changes in correctional facilities.[2]

Catch that? "Not hyperbole" and "nothing short of miraculous." Rare phrases to read in a report about a correctional facility. But that's not enough for some people.

"Why would an inmate sue you?" she asked.

I glanced through the lawsuit. "Because he hated his food so much he claims . . . we violated the Eighth Amendment . . . which says prisoners shall not be subjected to *cruel and unusual punishment*." I stifled a laugh and added, "Well, I sure hope teenagers across America don't figure out they can sue over not liking what's put on their plates."

Prisons lately have come under fire for not being sufficiently comfortable, especially now that lefties seem to run the prisons. Social justice warriors use the word *rehabilitative* because they believe that prison should help satisfy practical, intellectual, and spiritual needs through job training, educational initiatives, and other activities.

I don't buy that. When I took over the House of Corrections, I dug in deep. First, I looked at the GED program and discovered that the average reading level of all the inmates was at the seventh-grade level. I went to the college running the GED program and asked, "How many inmates who start the program in jail continue once they get out?" The House of Corrections was never intended to be an institution where inmates were kept for long durations.

"We don't know," they said. "We don't keep those kinds of records."

"What do you mean you don't know?" I asked. I was astounded. "So you get paid money to start the program in jail. But once they get released from jail, you could care less about them?"

Keep in mind sometimes judges make continuing education one of the stipulations of their sentencing. A criminal might be ordered to get a job, get a GED, not partake of drugs or alcohol, and have no further contact with the law. If the man doesn't continue to pursue his education, he's in violation of the sentencing order. But as I stood there, I realized no one was keeping up with this. Seventy percent of inmates end up right back in jail, and this guy falls through the cracks. No one cares; no one follows up. The fact of the matter was that these programs were not about helping these inmates get a GED. It was about getting paid for running a perpetual program in the jail. I ended this ineffective program.

Then I looked into the so-called job-training program, which, of course, looks good on paper. "What are we training them to do?" I asked. I knew we weren't training them to be electricians, plumbers, or steel workers. No, we were spending a great deal of money to prepare them to do low-paying, unskilled labor, exactly the type of training that an employer does upon hiring. For example, if an inmate went to a warehouse to get a job driving a forklift, the employer would provide forklift instruction. Or a former inmate could go to one of Milwaukee's many meat-packing plants that could always use unskilled labor. The processing plants have a tough time keeping workers because many think it's too cold. It'd be a great job for someone recently out of jail, and the employer would train him to do the dumping, grinding, and processing work. There's no way we could teach him that kind of stuff in jail.

Prison Isn't a Country Club

Prison isn't a country club, a university, or a spa. I really can't believe I have to point this out. It's a place where people are sent to be *disciplined*. I don't *want* my prisoners to kick back and be happy. I want them to feel so uncomfortable that they never want to darken the door again.

And I wasn't afraid to make it less comfy when I noticed the inmates lying around in bed all day and staying up late, harassing the guards. This night owl tendency probably got them in trouble in the first place. They kept ungodly hours and never could find employment because they were asleep during what you and I might call work hours.

"Lights off at 10:00 p.m.," I said when I took over. That meant lights out literally. There would be no card playing, nothing. The prisoners were welcome to stay up, but they'd be sitting in the dark. Then, in the morning, when productive people should be awake, I took the

mattresses off their beds. They were welcome to sleep on the uncomfortable wooden planks, but they weren't getting a mattress. If anyone
wanted to go to bed early, I put the mattresses back on the beds at 8:00
p.m. We repeated this process every day so the prisoners could get on
a schedule that could help their lives once they got out. That was one
way I was encouraging them to get into a more traditional lifestyle so
they could easily transition into society when they left.

Also while I was in charge of the correctional facility, the global
price of food skyrocketed. The cost of eggs, for example, went up 30
percent; milk rose 13 percent.[3] The price of our meals went up by 12
percent.[4] I began to look more closely at the menu and realized that
one item on their plates didn't absolutely need to be there: dessert.

When a local newspaper reporter was interviewing me for the
inevitable he's-so-mean story, I asked why people who have broken
society's rules should get dessert. I told the writer, "I don't get dessert
every day at home. As long as the taxpayers have to struggle with rising food costs and eat more Hamburger Helper, as long as they have
to adjust their living and eating habits, why should they have to pay
increased costs for people who have disregarded society's rules?"[5]

Everyone went crazy over this decision. But the criminals were just
as upset by what they *were* being served, even though all of my inmates
were getting nutritionally adequate meals with the proper vitamins and
proteins. We've come a long way in this nation from the bread-and-
water days when prisoners received only those basic rations until they
proved they were trustworthy enough to receive meat. Today's politically correct world questions using food as a deterrent for bad behavior,
and that's why I was being sued.

The meal in question was not mere bread and water. It was
Nutraloaf, made from various ingredients (depending on location) like
carrots, biscuit mix, a dairy blend, and cabbage. Nutraloaf has all of

the vitamins and minerals a human being needs, but the inmates don't love it. That's why I gave it only to inmates who had attacked inmates or my staff members.

It's not as bad as all the reporters make it out to be. I've eaten it. It's sort of like meatloaf. No, not the kind of meatloaf your mom used to make, but I'm nobody's mom. Nor am I the manager at Applebee's. After hearing of the lawsuit, a writer for the *Milwaukee Wisconsin Journal Sentinel* baked some and described it as "the devil's meatloaf"[6] that looked like a brick of dog vomit.

"The taste is not that horrible," he wrote. "Just enough so to remind you why it's wise to avoid incarceration whenever possible."

Exactly. You don't want to be in jail.

I just couldn't sit by and let violence occur inside the walls of my facility. No way. And it wasn't just a matter of safety. It was a matter of the bottom line: when unruly inmates attacked members of my staff, they had to take time off to recover, we had to pay other officers overtime to take the place of the injured employees, and our insurance premiums skyrocketed. Saving taxpayer money was important to me.

When Prude filed a lawsuit against me, claiming I was violating the Eighth Amendment, I was eager for my day in court. He wasn't a good guy who'd made a few mistakes. He was arrested for armed robbery, and the assistant district attorney explained that he was responsible for several threatening calls made from the jail to one of the robbery victims *after he'd been arrested*. His victim and the victim's family had to be put under witness protection.

His behavior caused the judge to lower the hammer on Mr. Prude. "The fact that one of the victims was contacted while this case was pending, whether it was by you or on your behalf, and told essentially not to testify was truly outrageous. It indicates, Mr. Prude, just how dangerous of an individual you are," he said. "That somehow you can think that even in the face of having robbed so many people you would continue to terrorize and try and intimidate people who did nothing more than get in your way."[7]

He was convicted of five counts of armed robbery and sentenced to eighty years of imprisonment followed by twenty years of probation.[8]

Did I care that this guy wasn't happy? No way! But the rest of society began studying Nutraloaf and its implications for prison life. I could've saved them some trouble because I saw the effects firsthand, and they were glorious.

The great thing about Nutraloaf is that I served it in the disciplinary pods for every meal for days or weeks. If you're up on a first-degree murder charge or a serious sexual assault of a child, you don't have much to lose in jail. But once we started giving them Nutraloaf for every meal, incidences of fights, disorderly conduct, and attacks against our staff dropped tremendously. The word got around as we knew it would.

"Please, please, I won't do that anymore," inmates often told us. "Don't put me in the disciplinary pod. I don't want to eat Nutraloaf."

Twenty-two loaf-related lawsuits had been filed over the previous two years, but all had failed.[9] Regrettably, the insurance company for Aramark, the producer of the loaf, gave Prude a five-figure settlement to make the lawsuit go away. And so, in the era of lawsuits, pampered prisoners, and political correctness, I didn't have my day in court.

In addition to the fight focused on food, I had to fight against government-funded drug rehabilitation. The district attorney in Milwaukee County, John Chisholm, decided he wanted to send fewer criminals to prison. As Professor Alfred Blumstein explained,

Criminal justice is a system, and no one person or group is in charge of it. You have legislators who decide what's a crime and establish the range of penalties. You have judges who impose the sentences. You have police who decide whom to arrest. And you have prosecutors who have wide discretion in what cases to bring, what charges to call for, and what sentences to agree to in plea bargains.[10]

Since most cases don't make it to court because they are negotiated via plea bargains, Chisholm was frequently making decisions about how long someone goes to prison. That's when he unilaterally decided to take a different course for people he deemed a low-level threat to society. He called it "early intervention," and it went something like this. Let's say the hard-working police officers in Milwaukee arrested a guy on the street for drugs. Before the guy was arraigned, Chisholm would ask a number of questions.

- Have you had two or more prior adult convictions?
- Have you been arrested before you are age sixteen?
- Are you currently unemployed?
- Do you have criminal friends?[11]

If he got a score that indicated low risk, Chisholm would put the criminal into what is called a "diversion," a sort of probation track that would allow him to emerge from it without a criminal record. If he got a score that was higher, Chisholm asked a more comprehensive set of questions:

- Were you ever suspended or expelled from school?
- Does your financial situation contribute to your stress?
- Tell me the best thing about your supervisor/teacher.

Depending on how the criminal scores, he might be put into "deferred prosecution," meaning he would have a record, but his charges might be reduced or dismissed if he also went to rehab.

I felt the district attorney needed to emerge from Candy Land and live in the real world before he did more social experimentation. By offering second, third, and fourth chances to criminals, the "Milwaukee Experiment" endangered the homes, neighborhoods, and schools of the people he said he wanted to protect. Government-funded drug rehab programs demotivate people from addressing their problems. Sending them to rehab instead of prison isolated offenders from the ramification of all of their choices. I didn't want taxpayers to pay for that. Criminals should find their own mental health solutions through the private sector, *before* committing crimes and putting the rest of us in danger.

Let's face it. Communities in which most crimes occur don't have support structures in place for social alternatives to incarceration. Consequently, it's not wise to put them back into the community to claim more black victims. If you want to let people back on the street, you have to think about the people who are going to be dealing with them. My people. Black people. Most criminal justice reform is normalizing criminal behavior in a community that can least afford it— the ghettos. Of course, white liberals feel better about themselves when they come up with these soft-on-crime policies, no matter the real-world consequences. Then they drive into their mostly white neighborhoods and sleep soundly in their comfortable, safe beds.

You might be wondering why a prosecutor would *want* to reduce the number of criminals who are put into prison. Isn't a prosecutor's job to, you know, prosecute? What's wrong with the "lock 'em up and throw away the key" mentality? The criminal justice system has a race problem, at least according to many politicians and social activists. And something *must* be done.

Here are the sad statistics. In Wisconsin, 6 percent of the general population is black; 37 percent of the prison population is black. In 2010, the University of Wisconsin-Milwaukee published a troubling study that showed Wisconsin with "the highest black male incarceration rate in the nation. In Milwaukee County over half of African American men in their 30s have served time in state prison."[12] The study, titled "Wisconsin's Mass Incarceration of African American Males," goes along with the national narrative being developed by our so-called political leaders: the criminal justice system has unfairly targeted black Americans, creating a "mass incarceration" of blacks.

The handwringing perhaps started when CNN's Christiane Amanpour asked Bill Clinton about his 1994 omnibus crime bill made famous for its federal "three strikes" provision. Under his plan, if a person was convicted of a violent felony after two or more previous convictions (including drug charges), he'd receive a mandatory life sentence.

"The problem is the way it was written and implemented is we cast too wide a net and we had too many people in prison," Clinton responded. "We wound up . . . putting so many people in prison that there wasn't enough money left to educate them, train them for new jobs and increase the chances when they came out so they could live productive lives."[13]

Mrs. Bill Clinton later echoed her husband's culpability: "I . . . have a very comprehensive approach towards fixing the criminal justice system," she said. "Going after systemic racism that stalks the justice system . . . and ending the incarceration of low level offenders."[14]

(Side note: Some have observed that I always refer to Hillary

Clinton as "Mrs. Bill Clinton," so allow me to explain. This woman is married to Bill Clinton in an attachment of convenience. Politically, she has been the benefactor of his name as First Lady of Arkansas, as First Lady of the United States, and as a carpetbagging senator of New York. Her husband carried her politically; she launched her political career using *his* name for political advantage. Good for her. It worked. But for the name of Bill Clinton, she would've achieved nothing politically. She knows it. That's why she protected his reputation when scores of women claimed Bill assaulted them. She knew how valuable that name would be to her down the road, so she didn't hesitate in trashing their reputations and—consequently—their lives. In her failed 2016 campaign for president, she used his name and even said he'd be in charge of fixing the economy. Now I will make her own that name because she is *not* a self-made woman. End of rant.)

But the epidemic of the lamented "mass incarceration of African Americans" extends beyond Mr. and Mrs. Bill Clinton. President Barack Obama, who has repeatedly said drug laws disproportionately punish black people, visited El Reno Federal Correctional Institution outside Oklahoma City, where he talked to six inmates who had been put in prison for drug offenses.

Just let that sink in. A sitting president went to a prison to lift the spirits of the inmates, to talk to people who have been engaged in criminal activity and have put the lives of law-abiding Americans at risk. I'm old enough to remember when presidents were *against* crime.

After his visit, a reporter asked him a softball question: What struck him the most by his visit?

"When they describe their youth and their childhood, these are young people who made mistakes that aren't that different than the mistakes I made and the mistakes that a lot of you guys made," he said. "The difference is they did not have the kinds of support structures, the second chances, the resources that would allow them to survive those mistakes."

It's almost as though you could be walking down the street smoking pot and end up in the pen, according to Obama, who said, "Over the last few decades, we've also locked up more and more nonviolent drug offenders than ever before, for longer than ever before. And that is the real reason our prison population is so high."[15] He went on to say that a disproportionate percentage of minorities were being imprisoned because of the War on Drugs and our nation's "long history of inequity in the criminal-justice system."

But this isn't just Democrat talking points; Republicans are into this game as well.

In March 2015, the Koch brothers teamed up with George Soros to sponsor the Bipartisan Summit on Criminal Justice Reform, hosted by conservative Newt Gingrich and liberal Van Jones. The gist of the conference attended by people of both parties was that our nation was locking up too many black people.

Perhaps Michelle Alexander, writing in *The New Jim Crow*, put the sharpest point on it: "Mass incarceration—not attacks on affirmative action or lax civil rights enforcement—is the most damaging manifestation of the backlash against the Civil Rights Movement."[16]

You got that? Again and again, you will hear that America is putting too many nonviolent blacks into prison, mostly because of insignificant drug issues. But this lie is getting people killed.

The anti-incarceration talking points are based on two major myths:

Myth #1: Recreational drug use has landed so many otherwise law-abiding citizens behind bars. The Manhattan Institute did an eye-opening study on this very issue and discovered that "less than 1 percent of federal prisoners have been convicted of drug possession, and most of those convictions were bargained down from serious trafficking charges."[17] Also, it's not easy to land in prison in this nation:

> Most convicted felons never reach prison, and those who do are typically repeat offenders guilty of the most serious violent and property crimes. The system sends very few people to prison for simple drug possession. Drug-related convictions do not disproportionately harm the black community. To the contrary, if all drug offenders were released tomorrow, there would be no change in the black share of prisoners. We do know, however, that putting the most dangerous criminals behind bars reduces victimization for crime-plagued communities. As the incarceration rate for violent felons has increased, crime rates have plunged, saving countless lives and improving public safety, especially in minority neighborhoods.[18]

The Manhattan Institute also found that 47 percent of Americans serving time behind bars are there because of violent crimes. Only 20 percent are there for drug-related crimes. You can't blame the drug laws on the high number of blacks in prison.

Myth #2: Racism is the driving force behind harsher sentencing, putting too many nonviolent blacks behind bars. During his time in office, President Obama could not stop talking about racist policing. When he went before the NAACP in Philadelphia, he said that

> there are costs that can't be measured in dollars and cents. Because the statistics on who gets incarcerated show that by a wide margin, it disproportionately impacts communities

of color. African Americans and Latinos make up 30 percent of our population; they make up 60 percent of our inmates. About one in every 35 African American men, one in every 88 Latino men is serving time right now. Among white men, that number is one in 214. The bottom line is that in too many places, black boys and black men, Latino boys and Latino men experience being treated differently under the law.[19]

After that last line, the members of the audience responded with thunderous applause. Remember when Obama's election was supposed to usher in an era of racial healing? Me neither.

But author and researcher Heather MacDonald demolished this myth when she testified before the Senate Judiciary Committee in 2015. She explained that this was perhaps one of the most dangerous inaccuracies:

> For decades, criminologists have tried to find evidence proving that the overrepresentation of blacks in prison is due to systemic racial inequity. That effort has always come up short. In fact, racial differences in offending account for the disproportionate representation of blacks in prison. A 1994 Justice Department survey of felony cases from the country's 75 largest urban areas found that blacks actually had a lower chance of prosecution following a felony than whites. Following conviction, blacks were more likely to be sentenced to prison, however, due to their more extensive criminal histories and the gravity of their current offense.[20]

I can tell you this from personal experience. If you go to a neighborhood riddled with crime, the people who live there don't want drug dealers and users to be put back on their streets. Who would? Residents of these neighborhoods want tougher sentencing, not more lenient sentencing. Only in the twisted logic of liberal class and race guilt would putting druggies back on the street seem like a good idea.

So why are there so many black people in prison?

No matter how complicated social activists try to make it out to be, no matter how much they try to blame society, cops, or whatever else, there are so many black people in prison because so many black people commit crimes.

Discipline, Order, Training, and Structure (DOTS)

I was in Target one day, and a black woman stopped me and said, "You're Sheriff Clarke." I get stopped frequently at stores, but I was not expecting what came next. She continued, "My son has been in and out of the House of Corrections ever since you took that over." I'm sure my back stiffened. The media didn't like my approach to prisoner comfort, and I'd gotten sick of all the criticism people hurled my way. "But he's out, and he told me he doesn't want to go back there."

"'Mom, Sheriff Clarke ain't playing no games,' he told me. 'He's running the jail the way it should be.'"

I breathed a sigh of relief. I expected her to lay into me and say I've been too hard on her son.

"Well, I try to instill a sense of discipline," I began, but just as I started talking, a young man walked up to us.

"Here comes my son now!" the mother exclaimed.

Uh-oh, I thought.

"Everything okay, Mom?" he asked. She'd been in the store longer than expected, so he'd come in to check on her. Even though she'd characterized him as appreciative of my reforms, you never know what you're going to get. However, I found him to be respectful and courteous to me.

Previously, inmates weren't really bothered about going to jail. They didn't like it, but they thought of it as a minor inconvenience. But my reforms made jail a very unpleasant place, just as it should be.

I don't know if that guy is going to walk the straight and narrow. But I had figured out a way to give people like him more of a chance. I had noticed that too many inmates leave jail, go home as the same dysfunctional people they were when they went in, and return to the same house and the same goofs for friends. As I mentioned before, inmates don't need another job program. They need a discipline program.

An employer needs someone who is reliable, trustworthy, prompt, respectful, and productive. But many of these individuals don't exhibit these qualities. Instead of teaching them some sort of low-paying skills, I decided to teach them something that could really help them: life skills.

In 2010, I created the Discipline, Order, Training, and Structure (DOTS) program to give offenders the tools necessary to make a cognitive decision to change their behavior so we don't see them back at the jail. We based this on a Michigan Department of Corrections' program, and I thought I'd finally found something that would get broad-based community and political support. After all, who's against teaching inmates life skills?

People from Michigan came to Milwaukee County and worked with a group I'd put together to run this program. My employees went to Michigan to see firsthand how this program runs. Instead of hiring people to run this program, I assigned the task to staff who were already with us so we didn't spend additional funds. The program would cost the taxpayers precisely $0 since I had already cut programs that didn't work in order to make room in my budget for this one.

I invited the reporter who covers county government to my office and laid out the whole program for him. I knew I'd be able to get public and political support with this innovative program that I hoped would help people get on track.

We began with one dormitory of sixty inmates who'd be given a few perks. They'd have access to a better quality of food with a bit more say-so in the menu. They wouldn't get filet mignon or lobster, but we would bring in hamburger meat on Wednesday night, opening up the kitchen and letting them cook the meat themselves. Also, they got to watch movies and cable television, which was a huge benefit for them. Men who were willing to go through my program would have more control over their lives, but they would have to have to earn it. Special privileges such as access to television or visitation could be revoked for infractions.

"This is strictly voluntary," we said, to the inmates before explaining what it would entail. The participants would get up at 5:00 a.m., take an early morning run, and then do fitness training, before focusing on their work detail, education, and job-training classes. There would also be a time of team competition so that they learned how to push one another to achieve group success. Lights out for this program was 9:30 p.m.

Other classes taught them basic life lessons. For example, I brought in an economist to explain how a dollar works and how to balance a checkbook. These guys didn't have a lot of money, and they wouldn't have a lot when they got out of jail. But they tended to let money go through their hands as soon as they had it—spending it on dope, potato chips, or whatever else. They had no sense of how money is supposed to work. I helped them understand that if you put a little away gradually, suddenly you might have an extra fifteen dollars.

The program was an astounding success. The participants—some of whom had never finished anything in their lives—received a certificate when they completed DOTS. Many of them had family and friends attend the graduation ceremony. You could see the sense of accomplishment etched on their faces. Some of them had not graduated from high school or even middle school. Going through this program gave them the chance to hold their heads up high, walk across the stage, and receive a diploma. It wouldn't magically change their lives.

"What you do with this is up to you," I said as I congratulated the men on their success.

One guy wrote me a letter that I've kept all these years:

The reason for this letter, sir, is to thank you. The DOTS program you came up with is brilliant, sir. It's helped me to become a better man in today's society. Being in this program has opened my eyes. When the captain described the program, I knew it was what I wanted—a change in my life and in my attitude . . . My life hasn't been the greatest, but not a lot of people's are. I made bad choices, had a bad attitude, and a bad outlook on life. This program let me see the error of my ways. It has also given me the tools to make a positive change.

What's even more impressive about the handwritten letter is that the guy wrote me on the very evening that he was scheduled to get out of jail, and he wanted to stay in longer:

Unfortunately, I leave tonight and I am sad to go. I asked the captain if I could stay past my outdate so I could continue the program and graduate. He told me I couldn't.

Isn't that astonishing? An inmate who would rather stay in jail for the program so he could keep learning and improving his life. The very personal, touching letter went on to say that his mother was recovering from cancer, so it would be good for him to get out of jail to take care of her. I've kept this letter to remind me that people's lives were changed through this program.

I'd like to tell you that conservatives and liberals all over Milwaukee welcomed this program, but that never happens, does it? The reporter I'd brought in—who even interviewed the people at the Michigan Department of Corrections—totally sabotaged what we were trying to do by using two words in his initial article: "Boot camp."

The words *boot camp* have a negative connotation with the Left, so suddenly all of the county supervisors were against my new program before it had barely begun.

Editorials showed up in the newspaper about my "Draconian measures." People complained that I'd taken the mattresses away from the inmates and said I gave them essentially bread and water. The political pressure to destroy the program I'd taken so much care to create was intense.

"We're not funding it," the county supervisors told me.

"I didn't ask for one penny," I shot back.

Then they threatened to cut the overall jail budget so we couldn't have it anymore. The entire time that I was trying to teach those guys how to balance a checkbook, I had to fight lefty politics. I felt as if I was roller-skating up a hill backward in my efforts to help those inmates.

Sometimes I get weary of the fight—the constant, nagging fight—but God knows when I need a little boost. When I get down about all of the criticism, that's when he places in my path someone like that woman I met in Target. Or I might receive a handwritten letter from an inmate whose life is back on track. Those moments remind me that even though I'm not perfect, my work is meaningful. I've actually been in the trenches helping to change these men's lives, no matter how many editorials accuse me of being mean and heartless.

Theodore Roosevelt's "The Man in the Arena" speech made in 1910 at the Sorbonne in France comes to mind:

It is not the critic who counts; not the man who points out how the strong man stumbles, or where the doer of deeds could have done them better. The credit belongs to the man who is actually in the arena, whose face is marred by dust and sweat and blood; who strives valiantly; who errs, who comes short again and again, because there is no effort without error and shortcoming; but who does actually strive to do the deeds; who knows great enthusiasms, the great devotions; who spends himself in a worthy cause; who at the best knows in the end the triumph of high achievement, and who at the worst, if he fails, at least fails while daring greatly, so that his place shall never be with those cold and timid souls who neither know victory nor defeat.

5

American Education Embraces and Enforces Poverty

FREDERICK DOUGLASS WAS BORN as a slave sometime around 1818 in Talbot County, Maryland. As a young child, he wondered why the white kids knew their actual birthdays, but he didn't. He also witnessed his Aunt Hester get savagely beaten after she fell in love with another slave. Like most in his situation, he grew up without a father; his mother died when he was ten years old.

That's when he was sent to Baltimore to serve the Auld family. Douglass described the matriarch of the household, Sofia, as a "kind and tender hearted woman," though she did require two things of the young slave. First, she made him stop cowering, improve his posture, and stand up straight. Second, she required him to look her in the eye when they spoke. For the first time in his life, Douglass was being treated like a human being. Soon, Sofia took a risk and began teaching him the alphabet.

At one time in this great country, it was against the law to educate "negroes" as they called them. Any attempt to educate slaves had to occur underground. The slave-owning culture of the South frowned upon masters teaching their slaves to read and write. The prevailing orthodoxy then was that education would open the eyes of slaves and incite rebellion toward their oppressors. Eventually they would demand their freedom. The following language appeared in the state of Virginia's Revised Code of 1819:

> That all meetings or assemblages of slaves, or free negroes or mulattoes mixing and associating with such slaves at any meeting-house or houses, &c., in the night; or at any SCHOOL OR SCHOOLS for teaching them READING OR WRITING, either in the day or night, under whatsoever pretext, shall be deemed and considered an UNLAWFUL ASSEMBLY; and any justice of a county, &c., wherein such assemblage shall be, either from his own knowledge or the information of others, of such unlawful assemblage, &c., may issue his warrant, directed to any sworn officer or officers, authorizing him or them to enter the house or houses where such unlawful assemblages, &c., may be, for the purpose of apprehending or dispersing such slaves, and to inflict corporal punishment on the offender or offenders, at the discretion of any justice of the peace, not exceeding twenty lashes.[1]

"Learning would spoil the best n— in the world," Douglass's master, Hugh Auld, said when he discovered his wife had been teaching him the alphabet. If Douglass learned to read, Mr. Auld warned his wife, he'd no longer be content to be merely a slave.

He was right about that last part. Though Mrs. Auld stopped teaching him the alphabet, Douglass realized education would be his path out of slavery. He bribed poor white children with bread for tutorials and devised clever games to trick the white children into teaching him how to read.

But he wasn't content with just reading. He realized that to escape slavery, he also needed to learn how to write. Over the years, he gradually taught himself how to do just that. After he accomplished that goal, neither he nor our country was ever the same.

Douglass, as you now know, turned out to be one of our nation's most prominent civil rights advocates, a powerful orator, and an eloquent abolitionist writer.

What Douglass realized but our politicians have yet to grasp is that education opens minds. It teaches people to think for themselves. It connects people to the past and prepares them for the future. Education has always been the vehicle for upward mobility in the United States. My parents understood the value of an education and poured what little money they had into providing me with a solid educational base. They knew that in a sometimes unfair and unjust world, I would have to be doubly prepared to overcome obstacles.

That's why I'm so disappointed in the way that modern politicians have neglected their moral obligation to help black children thrive educationally.

The situation is dire.

A Cycle of Failure

Never in the history of our nation have the wealthy and the poor had such different lives. There's a cycle of failure that I've seen too frequently in all of my years as a cop. Generations of black kids are functionally illiterate because their parents were functionally illiterate. It doesn't take an education specialist to predict that the next generation will be functionally illiterate as well. In a way, it's a self-inflicted pathology, but we taxpayers who support an inadequate government are responsible for it too. As long as the government ties the hands of parents, forcing them to keep their kids in failing public schools, how can we hold them responsible? Even black parents who are totally engaged with their children end up sending their kids to an inferior school system for lack of options. Kids get up every morning, go to school, and do their homework in the evenings. But once they've completed their education, they're unprepared for much in the real world.

University of Kansas researchers Betty Hart and Todd Risley studied the ways in which parents and children interact with one another and discovered what we're up against. They found the number of words heard by children varied greatly according to the social standing of the parents. Parents on welfare had half as much verbal interaction with their children than working-class parents had with theirs. High-income families interacted verbally with their kids the most. Children from families on welfare heard about 616 words per hour; children from working-class families heard around 1,251 words per hour; kids from professional families heard roughly 2,153 words per hour.[2]

The study also revealed that higher-income parents praised their kids more frequently than lower-income parents.

> Children from families with professional backgrounds experienced a ratio of six encouragements for every discouragement. For children from working-class families this ratio was two encouragements to one discouragement. Finally, children from families on welfare received on average two discouragements for every encouragement. Therefore, children from families on welfare seemed to experience more negative vocabulary than children from professional and working-class families.[3]

Another marked difference is obvious when it comes to reading. White parents are more likely to read to their kids before they tuck them into bed. Of parents with a college degree, 71 percent read to their children every day. Only 33 percent of parents with a high school diploma or less read to their kids daily.[4]

Imagine how that one difference affects lower-income kids. They do not show up to school in a state of educational readiness. Teachers can teach, but they can't perform miracles for the poorer children from such disadvantaged backgrounds. The level of education determines how much money the children will be able to earn later in life. Poor kids receive less education and—consequently—earn less money.

And the cycle continues.

Failing Families

How do you think the United States ranks in overall education compared to the rest of the world? Number one? Top ten? Not even close. In 2014, we were twenty-ninth, behind Russia, Vietnam, and the Slovak Republic. Every day, on average, seven thousand students drop out of high school, bringing the annual tally to 1.2 million kids.[5]

Take a look at Milwaukee Public School District, the largest in the state of Wisconsin. The State Department of Public Instruction graded the district with an F. Only 18 percent of black Milwaukee kids tested proficiently at reading, and their graduation rate was 59 percent. That is a poor return for the very high price tag of $1.1 billion.[6]

Families frequently choose where they live to make sure they're zoned for the right school district, but what if you can't afford to live in the vicinity of the better schools?

School choice gives parents who want to get their kids out of a failing school system a lifeline. Why would anyone want to interfere with parents trying to help their kids? In the year 2017, we shouldn't be putting parents on a list to get their kids into grade school. It seems medieval. School choice allows public education funds to be used for schools that best fit students' needs—whether that's public school, private school, home school, or charter school.

Publicly funded charter schools are free from many rules and regulations of other public schools. Frequently, charters receive more applications than they have desks available, so they use a lottery to decide which students get into the school. Charter schools substantially outperform traditional public schools. According to Timothy Benson at *National Review*:

- Charter schools close racial achievement gaps, for example, at a much higher rate than do traditional public schools.
- New York charters easily outpace traditional public schools in math and English language arts.
- The student bodies of New York charters are comprised of 92 percent minorities, and these institutions account for 38 percent of the top fifty schools in the city.
- Charters suspend students at lower rates than neighboring public schools.[7]

To our great national shame, however, the opening of charter schools has become a political issue. In 2016, the NAACP passed a resolution calling for a pause on privately managed charter schools. It claimed charter schools "increase segregation," use "disproportionately high" levels of "punitive and exclusionary discipline," and could have "psychologically harmful environments." Even worse, it said that charter schools are spreading in "low-income communities" just like "predatory lending practices that led to the sub-prime mortgage disaster."[8]

What? *Targeting* low-income areas and communities of color?

Let's think about this a second. Why would charter schools open in black neighborhoods? Because that's where schools have failed. That's where they're needed. One size doesn't fit all in education reform, and our K-12 school system was designed for a different century. We need to give parents every opportunity to make sure their kids are educated. The NAACP should be investigating this abject failure instead of opposing the one program that is advantageous to black children.

For the nation's most premier civil rights organization to oppose charter schools because they're opening at a higher rate in inner cities is the height of lunacy. Does anyone really believe that charter schools create "psychologically harmful environments" when these schools are voluntary—frequently with long waiting lists? Benson put it nicely:

> If the NAACP truly wants to help black children, it should pass a resolution affirming that black parents should have the freedom to choose the schools their children attend and should not be penalized financially for choosing a private school, whether religious or secular. Empirical evidence shows that school-choice programs work, and polls show that they are broadly popular. In a poll taken in January, the American Federation for Children found that 65 percent of parents support private-school choice, 75 percent support public charter schools, 65 percent support education savings accounts, and 53 percent support school vouchers. All forms of school choice, public and private, should be on the table for the NAACP. The goals for the NAACP should be not only school choice for every black parent but, for every school educating black children, the requirement that it compete—and for every black child, an opportunity to attend a quality school.[9]

Charter schooling is just one way that black parents can be empowered to educate their children. If charter schools aren't available in a child's neighborhood, vouchers give parents the option of choosing a private school. Under such a program, funds typically spent by a school district on the child would be given to a participating family through a voucher system that could be used to pay partial or full private school tuition.

My hope is that these options could get poorer kids into schools that don't promote kids regardless of whether they learn to read.

Whenever I bring up the controversial topic of social promotion, people ask me, "Well, we can't flunk all these kids, can we?"

I always respond in the same way: "Why are you asking me? I'm just a cop." But I guarantee, I see the consequences of our failed public schools more than anyone else. On the streets, I see kids who are stuck in this perpetual cycle of poverty and crime; they never seemed to really have a chance. My thirty-eight years on the police force tell me that if something doesn't work, you stop doing it. Heck, I probably understood that when I was just a kid. What if parents started suing these school systems for not making good on their promise to educate their kids? Is that what it will take to get their attention?

Reading, 'Riting, and Undermining
Our National Greatness

Although schools these days fail at educating our kids, they succeed in indoctrinating them. We used to regard schools as places where children were sent to learn about our country, our values, our shared heritage, and our collective knowledge. Now teachers are instructing children that they need to radically transform the nation. Schools are no longer institutions of learning. They are laboratories of progressive indoctrination. Encouraging critical thought has been replaced by demanding regurgitation of leftist ideology to get a passing grade. These days, students know how to address the transgendered with the proper pronouns, but they aren't able to do basic math. Textbooks emphasize America's failures and minimize our accomplishments.

The great Thomas Sowell pointed out that this phenomenon is not new or even unique to America:

> In France between the two World Wars, the teachers' union decided that schools should replace patriotism with internationalism and pacifism. Books that told the story of the heroic defense of French soldiers against the German invaders at Verdun in 1916 despite suffering massive casualties were replaced by books that spoke impartially about the suffering of all soldiers—both French and German—at Verdun. Germany invaded France again in 1940, and this time the world was shocked when the French surrendered after just six weeks of fighting—especially since military experts expected France to win. But two decades of undermining French patriotism and morale had done their work.[10]

Why are American schools undermining our nation's greatness? I don't think it's hyperbole to say that today's black Americans are in a similar position as Frederick Douglass when he was a kid. An inept government has once again made it all too difficult for black people to learn. It's time for us to focus on improving education with as much passion as the abolitionists had when fighting to eliminate slavery. Failing, misguided schools are entrapping black children into a lifetime of missed opportunities and mediocrity.

As Douglass wrote, "Where justice is denied, where poverty is enforced, where ignorance prevails, and where any one class is made to feel that society is an organized conspiracy to oppress, rob and degrade them, neither persons nor property will be safe."

It's time to demand better, America.

6

How Lies Turned Isolated Deaths into National Scandals

A BLACK MOTHER put a Harvard bumper sticker on the back of her son's Toyota Corolla.

"You must be proud," another woman said.

"Oh he goes to the local community college," the black mother said. "This is so the cops won't rough him up when they pull him over."

For the past few years, whenever you've turned on the television or looked online, one narrative has constantly been hammered into our minds: black people better watch their backs because racist cops are just around the corner waiting to entrap them. To combat this fear, black moms and dads sit their kids down and have "the talk." Since innocent traffic stops can get black kids killed, they have to know a few tricks: keep your hands on the steering wheel, don't reach for anything inside your pockets, say "yes sir" and "no sir," let the police officer know he's in charge.

The only problem? This notion is based on a myth.

In chapter 3, we learned that most people who died during a police interaction were wielding weapons, suicidal, mentally troubled, or running when officers told them to stop. In other words, an innocent black man most likely won't be killed by a racist cop. Period. That's not my wishful thinking. That's a reasonable conclusion based on evidence.

So why are parents scaring their children and creating distrust of the one group putting their lives on the line for their communities every day? Because the stories about race that dominate the news are, more often than not, utter fabrications. Yes, even the most famous cases. By now, the names of black people killed by whites are household names—Trayvon Martin, Michael Brown, Eric Garner, and Tamir Rice—but the real stories are much more complicated than what you've read or heard. Let's take a closer look beyond the headlines and hashtags at what's really happening in America.

Trayvon Martin

On February 26, 2012, a seventeen-year-old black high school student named Trayvon Martin was walking through the neighborhood where he was temporarily living when he crossed paths with twenty-eight-year-old neighborhood watchman George Zimmerman. Even though the kid hadn't broken any laws and was unarmed, he wound up dead.

This incident didn't involve police, yet it became a modern parable of how hard it is to be a black man in this nation. This is why a mother puts a Harvard bumper sticker on her son's car and why a father sits his son down for "the talk." As images of a young hoodie-wearing Trayvon started showing up all over the media, President Obama famously said, "If I had a son, he would look like Trayvon."

This story was already tragic, but the media wanted it to be more—a hate crime, an incident that would further inflame racial tension in America—and here's how they did it.

First, they muddled Zimmerman's race. "George is a Spanish-speaking minority with many black family members and friends," said his Jewish father in describing the son he fathered with a Peruvian woman. Most would call Zimmerman Hispanic, but CNN described him as a "*white* Hispanic." You can call him half-Jewish maybe or half-Peruvian, but you can't call him white unless you're color-blind. If you saw him in real life instead of on TV, you could see that his skin is brown. However, his brother complained to NPR that many photos of Zimmerman making their way around the Internet mysteriously showed George with lighter skin than he actually has. The media intentionally tried to make him look whiter because it's hard to sell a racial narrative without an evil white man attacking an innocent black man.

Second, they muddled Martin's age. At the time of his death, Martin was just seventeen. As soon as the media began reporting the incident, however, they used a photo of him around the age of twelve. Though the death of a teenager is just as tragic as the death of a preteen, the media were desperate to shove the details of this real-life event into the mold of the racial narrative they wanted to tell. The younger the victim, the better. Reality didn't matter.

Third, they purposely made it look like racial profiling. When NBC aired the 911 call, the viewers of the *Today* show heard these words: "This guy looks like he's up to no good . . . he looks black." But what did those three dots represent? What was left out? The 911 operator asking Zimmerman, "Is he white, black, or Hispanic?"[1] Only then did Zimmerman mention race.

Fourth, they put on trial the "stand your ground" principle, which liberals hate because it authorizes people to protect themselves against perceived threats. When discussing this case, the media reported that

Zimmerman wasn't arrested because of the "stand your ground" principle, but that was not true. Even when Zimmerman had his day in court, his lawyers argued traditional self-defense.

Last, they made Martin into a martyr. If you read any coverage of this case, you may have seen the comparison between Martin and Emmett Till, a black man in Mississippi who was viciously murdered for whistling at a white woman during the 1950s. That was an absolute assault on history. But it was not as crazy as MSNBC personality Al Sharpton (no, I won't call him reverend) comparing the death of Trayvon Martin to the crucifixion of Jesus Christ.[2]

The media wanted a racial parable, so that's what we got. Rarely has such an incident penetrated the minds and hearts of Americans in politics, the academy, pop culture, and even sports. For example, the entire Miami Heat basketball team—including Dwyane Wade and LeBron James—posed for photos wearing hoodies, with their hands stuffed in their pockets. #WeWantJustice was one of the hashtags captioning the photo.

The only problem was that the story wasn't true. Zimmerman said Martin "sucker-punched" him and broke his nose. Witnesses testified that Martin was attacking Zimmerman before the shot was fired. A neighbor said Martin was attacking Zimmerman like a mixed martial arts fighter. A forensic expert testified that the end of his gun was right against Martin, which indicates that Martin had gotten on top of Zimmerman.[3]

You may not have heard these details espoused by a legal pro like LeBron James, but Zimmerman was ultimately found not guilty in a court of law. The verdict sent shock waves through this nation. The NAACP posted a petition asking the Department of Justice to open a civil case against Zimmerman, and within three days 1.5 million people had signed it.[4] Zimmerman's parents weren't able to return to their home because they feared for their lives. When the telephone number of a woman in Winter Park, Florida, was erroneously published as Zimmerman's number, death threats inundated her. The Seminole County Sheriff's Department could commiserate because it was receiving four hundred threats per minute via social media.

But that was just the beginning.

Michael Brown

On August 9, 2014, a white police officer in Ferguson, Missouri, shot an eighteen-year-old black man. The story about the shooting was seemingly custom made for the shame-the-police narrative. Michael Brown had robbed a convenience store of small cigars before a white cop found him and ended up shooting the unarmed man in the back. The media stories told us repeatedly that this kid had his entire life before him. He was preparing to go to college in the fall. Even worse, he was reportedly killed when he had his hands in the air, in a gesture of helpless surrender.

"Hands up, don't shoot" became a mantra for protestors on the street and social media. Violent protests, vandalism, and looting erupted in the mostly black city for more than a week. Police had to set a nightly curfew as beauty parlors and convenience stores burned to the ground. Americans turned on their televisions at night and saw images of tear gas, police in riot gear, sirens blazing, fires burning—all this evoking the race riots of the 1960s. Missouri's governor called in the National Guard and implied that the "prosecution" of the officer was the only way to achieve justice in this situation.

"Ferguson" became shorthand for all that is wrong with America. Political activists and politicians converged on the city like vultures on a roadside carcass. If you had taken a map of Missouri and asked these activists to point out the city of Ferguson, I bet 95 percent of them wouldn't have come close. But after the shooting, the town became ground zero, the epicenter of the police use of deadly force.

Again, there was a major problem. The story was not true.

Michael Brown, who'd robbed a convenience store just moments before his fateful run-in with the police, was no "gentle giant." When the store clerk tried to stop him from taking cigarillos, he shoved the clerk in a not-so-gentle way.

Then when Officer Darren Wilson saw Brown and his friend walking down the middle of the street, he blocked them with his vehicle and told them to move to the side. This interaction got violent fast when Brown and Wilson struggled for control of the officer's weapon until it fired. When Brown and his friend took off, the officer pursued them. Brown then turned around and came at the cop.

The autopsy revealed Brown had enough tetrahydrocannabinol, the main ingredient found in cannabis, to cause hallucinations and paranoia. Furthermore, Brown was *not* shot in the back. Blood splatters show that Brown was coming at the officer, not running away from him. By the way, his hands *weren't even raised* when he was killed. Several black witnesses confirmed what the autopsy and forensic evidence proved, but they had to remain in hiding because of the violence.

Let these details sink in. Almost everything you heard about that case was a lie.

Eric Garner

This might be the most heart-wrenching story of them all. In August 2014, the forty-three-year-old was illegally selling single cigarettes on the street in Staten Island. When New York City police officer Daniel Pantaleo approached him, Eric Garner waved his arms and said, "Every time you see me you want to arrest me. I'm tired of this, this stops today . . . I didn't do nothing . . . I'm minding my business, officer . . ."

That's when Pantaleo put Garner in what has been described as a headlock. Millions of Americans shuddered in horror as they saw the video of him lying on the ground, surrounded by officers. "I can't breathe," he said eleven times before having a fatal cardiac arrest.

Once again, America was thrust into national grief. #ICantBreathe trended on Twitter, and protestors shouted it on streets in major cities across America. NBA stars LeBron James, Kevin Garnett, Kyrie Irving, Deron Williams, and Derrick Rose warmed up in black "I Can't Breathe" T-shirts to show support for Garner's family. (The NBA decided not to fine the players for not wearing Adidas, which con-tractually provides the pregame warm-up clothing for players.) Of course, the perpetually aggrieved charlatan Sharpton descended to protest and lead a candlelight vigil.

Eventually the police were not indicted. The medical examiner said the cause of death was "compression of neck (choke hold), com-pression of chest and prone positioning during physical restraint by police." The autopsy said that his acute and chronic bronchial asthma, heart disease, and obesity were other factors (Garner weighed four hundred pounds) and that his windpipe had not been damaged.

When the officer was not indicted, cries of racism rang out through the nation. Again.

Tamir Rice

In November 2014, a citizen called 911 because he saw a person who scared him by waving around a gun in a Cleveland park. He told the emergency operator that the weapon was "probably fake," and the gun wielder was possibly a juvenile. The police responded to the call but were told only that it was a "code 1" situation—which meant it was of the highest priority and possibly posed significant risk to the public—and that there was a black man "wearing a camouflage hat and a gray jacket with black sleeves" waving a gun around and pointing it at people in the park.

When they pulled up, they saw Tamir Rice. He was not a man waving a gun, but a twelve-year-old boy waving a gun replica. It was an airsoft gun from which he had removed the orange tip that would've indicated it was fake. The video that immediately was seen by millions of Americans shows the cops pulling up and one of them shooting Tamir within seconds. Both police officers said they told him to put his hands up. Instead, Tamir reached for the gun in his waistband. He died the next day from the wounds.

"White police officer shoots and kills black child with a toy gun" was the dominant media narrative, and the cries of racial injustice only intensified when a Staten Island grand jury decided not to indict the officer. New York City Mayor Bill de Blasio went to a microphone and insinuated that the NYPD is full of racists. De Blasio, who has a biracial kid named Dante, said that he warned his son to "take special care" when interacting with police.

A Few Important Things to Note About Cops

I could go on. By the time you read this chapter, more racial incidents involving the police may be dominating the news. I hope not. But there are important lessons to be learned from these four incidents that the media certainly won't tell you.

Lesson 1. *When a law enforcement officer gives you a lawful command, obey it even if you disagree.* Whatever problem you are experiencing is not going to be settled on the street. People with complaints need to use the process established for that purpose. Though the cops don't have the final say, they have the final say *in the moment* within the law.

Think about how this basic principle could've affected the outcome of each case I just discussed.

Eric Garner didn't think he had to obey the police. "You're under arrest. Put your hands behind your back," they told him. All he had to do was turn around and put his hands behind his back. That one motion would've saved his life, and he'd be telling his story today about how he was hassled on the street by NYPD.

Michael Brown didn't think he had to obey the police when Officer Wilson told him, "Get out of the street." Is walking down the middle of the street a huge deal? No, and had Brown just gotten out of the street—even if he mumbled under his breath his disdain for the cop—he would be alive right now.

Tamir Rice didn't think he had to obey the cops when they yelled, "Put your hands up." Instead, he reached for what turned out to be a fake gun. Tragically, that decision cost this young boy his life.

Now, can some cops be overbearing and rude? For sure. But the bottom line is this: do what the officer tells you to do and then file a complaint if you need to.

Lesson 2. *Take politicians' words with a grain of salt.* President Barack Obama's first message to black Americans should've been this life-saving principle: don't attack a police officer on the street or resist arrest because you think you're being hassled. Instead, what did I hear? The president said that our police officers are poorly trained and have a fear of people who don't look like them. He said our police need more training to "be aware of their biases ahead of time."[5]

Disgusting.

United States Attorney General Eric Holder was also unhelpful when he chimed in, "We're gonna end racial profiling once and for all." Then he went to Ferguson and started making comments that communicated he already had his mind made up before a trial had commenced. He said, "This is a racist police organization." While he was in Ferguson, he visited with the grieving family of Michael Brown. That wasn't a bad thing in and of itself, but might that visit have colored his judgment? And I probably don't have to tell you that he didn't meet with Officer Wilson.

You expect race hustlers like Sharpton to talk stupid. But it really chapped my rear end when our nation's president, its attorney general, and even the mayor of New York City started spewing such incendiary rhetoric.

I was in Milwaukee when I heard about Mayor de Blasio's careless comments to his biracial son, and I had to take a moment to collect myself. Men and women in this profession put on their uniforms every day, go out on the streets to make their communities better, and 99.9 percent of them provide law and order for black people. The overwhelming majority of people living in these ghettos are good, law-abiding black people just trying to get through life without getting shot or having their kids killed by drug dealers controlling the streets. Think of what would happen in these cities if the police pulled back. Mayor de Blasio should have to experience New York City for just forty-eight hours with no police. The city would disintegrate into utter chaos.

Instead of speaking truth into the situation for all Americans, these politicians seized the opportunities to score cheap political points with certain demographics.

Lesson 3. *Bad laws make the cops look bad.* When police officers were enforcing the pedestrian ordinance in Ferguson, reporters and pundits quipped that apparently "walking the street in Ferguson" is a big crime now. Although it is a shame that Michael Brown ended up dead, just about every city in America has a pedestrian ordinance for a reason. The streets were made for cars; drivers shouldn't have to dodge pedestrian traffic.

But even *if* the pedestrian ordinances were too strict, the cops didn't pass them. If citizens don't like a law, they can go to the city council and say, "Rescind this ordinance." They can pass around petitions and write editorials in the local newspaper. That, however, is not the job of police officers. They are told to *enforce* the laws with sound judgment and discretion. They enforce the laws even when the laws aren't good.

This applies to Eric Garner in a very specific and tragic way. Remember, police stopped him for the very trivial crime of selling "loosies" (untaxed cigarettes) out of their packages. Usually they go for seventy-five cents per cigarette, or two for a dollar, but what created the very high demand for loosies? The smuggled cigarette trade is growing exponentially in New York City because there's a lot of money to be made and saved.

In the state of Virginia, cigarettes are taxed at around $0.30 per pack. In New York City, they're taxed at $5.85. Instead of the market setting the price for a pack, a law on the books sets a minimum price for a pack of premium-brand cigarettes in New York at $10.50. Oh, and the law prohibits coupons from moving the price below that price tag. Most packs even out at $12.50. People who smoke a pack a day can save a couple hundred dollars per month by purchasing out-of-state cigarettes. Plus, it's not illegal to have a couple of cartons of out-of-state cigarettes. It's just illegal to sell them in the city. That means there's a lot of temptation to buy untaxed cigarettes, and a lot of incentive to sell them. This creates an endless game of whack-a-mole for local authorities trying to keep up with the ever-changing set of rules.[6] It's no secret that up to 60 percent of cigarettes sold in the five boroughs are done so illegally.

Eric Garner died while taking advantage of the large demand for untaxed cigarettes. I think the triviality of that crime hit many Americans hard. All he was doing was selling cigarettes. Why couldn't the cops just leave him alone?

Because it's not the cops' duty to decide which laws to enforce.

Jack Dunphy, writing for *National Review*, put it best: "It's unfortunate that NYPD officers have been pressed into service as enforcers for the nanny state that New York City has become, but don't put a law on the books if you don't want the cops to enforce it, and don't ask them to enforce it if you're not willing to accept the fact that violence will sometimes occur when people resist that enforcement."[7]

Bill de Blasio should think about this before he insinuates that police departments are cesspools of racism, especially since the very laws he's shoving down the throats of New Yorkers contributed more to Eric Garner's death than that so-called choke hold.

7

Black Lives Matter Less to BLM
than Lies & Leftist Politics

AS I WROTE IN CHAPTER 3, Alica Garza was one of the founders of Black LIES Matter, but I think it would be insightful to look at that story more closely. On the night George Zimmerman was acquitted of killing of Trayvon Martin, Garza was drinking with her husband at an Oakland, California, bar.

"The whole bar went quiet," she told *California Sunday* magazine. "It felt like a gut punch, you know?"

She then went to Facebook to express her frustration. She posted a long "love letter to black people," which ended with "Black people. I love you. I love us. Our lives matter."

Her friend Patrisse Cullors saw the post and started using the hashtag #BlackLivesMatter under her own posts. The two friends then brought on Opal Tometi, and together, the three of them began the #BlackLivesMatter movement, with the hashtag moving beyond their circle of friends and starting to be used by a broader audience. It didn't become a movement until after Michael Brown was shot and killed in

Ferguson. Over the next few weeks, the slogan trended on social media nationally, uniting many Americans concerned over racial strife.

And you know the rest of the story. #BlackLivesMatter has been described as the most successful social media turned real-life movement in history. I guess that depends on your definition of *successful*.

Garza, Cullors, and Tometi were upset with the verdict in the Martin case, but why would we listen to their outrage instead of the six women jurors who heard all of the evidence and deliberated more than fifteen hours? Suffice it to say that being angry doesn't mean the snap legal assessment you made while sipping tequila in an Oakland bar is legally accurate. Eventually, the jurors decided Zimmerman was justified in his use of deadly force against Trayvon, which they described as "necessary to prevent imminent death or great bodily harm" to himself.

In the Michael Brown case, a grand jury heard testimony of forty eyewitnesses and then refused to indict Officer Darren Wilson. Turns out, many witnesses had been afraid to come forward with what they saw because the community was so angry. In the calmer courtroom, they were able to fully describe the events that transpired. The jurors also got to hear from forensic experts who showed that Brown wasn't shot as he was surrendering with his hands up. The DNA bloodstain evidence and witnesses' accounts didn't support the entire #HandsUpDontShoot mantra.

Wilson was exonerated of criminal wrongdoing later when the US Department of Justice (DOJ) released an extensive analysis of the shooting's ballistic, crime-scene, and eyewitness accounts. Investigators even went to the trouble of canvassing an additional three hundred homes in the neighborhood, trying to locate and interview more witnesses. Ultimately, the DOJ cleared the officer of violating Brown's civil rights, and—once again—deduced that his use of force was defensible. Eric H. Holder described the report as "fair and rigorous from the start." He said, "The facts do not support the filing of criminal charges against Officer Darren Wilson in this case." Perhaps anticipating the inevitable protests, he told doubters, "I urge you to read this report in full."[1]

I tell you the story of the origins of the movement because I want you to see how Martin's and Brown's deaths catalyzed it, especially now that we know what we know about how those court proceedings turned out.

So how did this exoneration affect Officer Wilson? Did America embrace him with open arms? Did Black LIES Matter condemn all of the racist, vile threats against him? Not quite. Racial tension and violent threats followed him no matter where he went. Some police-supporting Americans raised money for the officer so that he could pay his legal bills and buy a house on a dead-end street outside St. Louis, but he didn't put his name on the deed. Now he so fears for his safety that most of his friends don't know where he lives. When his wife got pregnant, people threatened to harm his unborn baby. She didn't check into the hospital under her own name when it was time to deliver the baby. Plus, Wilson is basically unemployable. The Ferguson Police Department told him that allowing him back on the force would endanger their current officers. Other police departments told him the same thing. With no other options, he resorted to selling boots at a retail store. But soon enough, reporters found him. After they kept calling the store, he left the job after only two weeks.[2]

It's sobering for people who wear the uniform to see Officer Wilson's life now. Here's a guy who had committed himself to serving the poorest communities, broke no laws, and was exonerated of all wrongdoing. Yet his life has been forever marred by an interaction that lasted less than two minutes. Remember when America wasn't led by mob rule or emotional rhetoric, but by the rule of law?

Here's the truth. Police aren't afraid of walking the streets or being shot by random criminals. They're afraid of being involved in an incident that would label them forever as trigger-happy racists. Wouldn't it be nice if police officers were judged not by social media and ham-fisted politicians, but by the laws they try so hard to enforce?

Black LIES Matter is not your grandfather's civil rights movement. It's the illegitimate child of these debunked racial incidents and the spawn of radical leftist activists. The founders of this movement have more in common with David Duke than Martin Luther King Jr. Yes, I mean that.

The organization is based on radical ideology and run by radical ideologues. Alicia Garza, Patrisse Cullors, and Opal Tometi were activists long before they took advantage of racial strife to propel themselves onto the national stage. Let's first take a look at the founders.

Garza is a queer woman who met and married a biracial transgendered man. (I'm too old school to understand how that works, so don't ask me.) Garza met Cullors on a dance floor in Rhode Island when they were attending a political "organizing" conference. Cullors came out of the closet when she was a teenager.

I point out their sexuality not because gay or transpeople can't have good ideas. Rather, I believe their radical ideology goes much deeper than seeking so-called justice for black Americans. These women are not your ordinary, run-of-the-mill people who are sick and tired of the way the world is. They're radical activists who hold values that most Americans don't share—that most *black* Americans don't share. It should come as no surprise to you that they are opposed to the nuclear family. Instead, they propose raising children through a black "village."

From the Black LIES Matter website:

We are committed to disrupting the Western-prescribed nuclear family structure requirement by supporting each other as extended families and "villages" that collectively care for one another, and especially "our" children to the degree that mothers, parents and children are comfortable.[3]

Note that they don't mention "fathers" in that utopian village. Only "mothers" and "parents" exist in their fantasy.

But wait, wasn't this whole thing based on outrage over the deaths of black men? Martin and Brown? Haven't they accused the American police officer of devaluing the lives of black men? Then, why are black men so marginalized on their website and in their visions for a better nation?

Because celebrating, promoting, and valuing the black lives of men were never their goal. Their goal is to spread radical leftist racism and hatred. The founders were involved in radical political activism long before Black LIES Matter. Garza was a political activist for "fair housing," "transgendered rights," and other leftist causes. She openly admires Marxist revolutionary Assata Shakur, a former Black Panther and convicted cop killer.[4] (In 1979, she escaped to Cuba with the help of the Black Liberation Army and radical Weather Underground Organization.)

Cullors promotes "social justice" in inner cities, fights incarceration, and engages in LBGTQ activism. She calls herself a "freedom fighter" and wants to so radically reduce the law enforcement budget that some departments would be entirely "disbanded or abolished."[5]

Tometi is a student of black liberation theology and an immigration activist who has said that "the racist structures that have long oppressed Black people" propagate a "cycle of oppression [that] is often ignored or dismissed by broader US society" and that "allows law enforcement to kill Black people at nearly the same rate as Jim Crow lynchings."[6]

It should surprise exactly no one that the founders' radicalism is also the cornerstone of the movement. This was most obvious when a group of sixty Black LIES Matter organizations served Hillary Clinton and Donald Trump—the two presidential candidates in 2016—a list of demands.

They demanded that the government should:

1. Get Rid of the Death Penalty

Their website, "The Movement for Black Lives," described this demand:

The death penalty is morally repugnant. The death penalty in the U.S. was designed to bring lynching into the courtroom and has targeted Blacks and other people of color and poor people throughout its history. The death penalty devalues Black lives—statistically those convicted of killing white people are at least three to four times more likely to be sentenced to death than killers of anyone else. The death penalty is also geographically discriminatory (about 1 percent of U.S. counties produce more than half of the death sentences), expensive (even more costly than life in prison without parole), and has resulted in innocent people being sentenced to death (156 people and counting are confirmed to date) and some even executed. It is randomly and arbitrarily sought by prosecutors who have the sole discretion to seek or not seek death, upwards of 95 percent of whom are white. The death penalty requires a high level of counsel, skill and resources not available to most defendants. We do not believe the death penalty was designed to be fair nor can it be fairly applied.[7]

2. Offer Free College Tuition
and Living Expenses to Blacks

"The Movement for Black Lives" described why this is fair:

Reparations for the systemic denial of access to high quality educational opportunities in the form of full and free access for all Black people (including undocumented and currently and formerly incarcerated people) to lifetime education including: free access and open admissions to public community colleges and universities, technical education (technology, trade and agricultural), educational support programs, retroactive forgiveness of student loans, and support for lifetime learning programs.[8]

3. Pass Legislation to Acknowledge
the Systemic Effects of Slavery

Slavery ended in 1865. The Jim Crow laws ended separate but equal discrimination with the passage of the Civil Rights Act of 1964—an act possible only by support of the majority of Republicans in Congress as President Lyndon Johnson had to contend with the majority of Democrats trying to defeat it. Remember that most of the members of Black LIES Matter movement weren't born in the 1960s, let alone the

1860s. They haven't experienced the harsh racism that pervaded the culture in real ways in either era.

These activists have no real grievance with our nation, but it didn't stop them from asking for this:

> Legislation at the federal and state level that requires the United States to acknowledge the lasting impacts of slavery, establish and execute a plan to address those impacts. This includes the immediate passage of H. R. 40, the "Commission to Study Reparation Proposals for African-Americans Act" or subsequent versions which call for reparations remedies.[9]

Nothing more than a movement of extortion. They want something they did not earn.

4. Give Black People Education Initiatives

The cradle-to-college pipeline has been systematically cut off for Black communities. According to the National Center for Education Statistics, 23 states spend more per pupil in affluent districts than in high-poverty districts that contain a high concentrations of Black students; and the U.S. Department of Education's Office of Civil Rights shows persistent and glaring opportunity gaps and racial inequities for Black students. Black students are less likely to attend schools that offer advanced coursework, less likely to be placed in gifted and talented programs, more likely to attend schools with less qualified educators, and employ law enforcement officers but no counselors. Public universities, colleges, and technical education remain out of reach for most in the United States and policies to help students cover costs continue to shift towards benefiting more affluent families.[10]

5. Provide Free Mental Health Counseling

That's not all. The Black LIES Matter crowd believes that it is so hard to live in America that they need counseling to deal with their day-to-day trauma:

> Reparations for the wealth extracted from our communities through environmental racism, slavery, food apartheid, housing discrimination and racialized capitalism in the form of corporate and government reparations focused on healing ongoing physical and mental trauma, and ensuring our access and control of food sources, housing and land.
>
> Reparations for the cultural and educational exploitation, erasure, and extraction of our communities in the form of mandated public school curriculums that critically examine the political, economic, and social impacts of colonialism and slavery, and funding to support, build, preserve, and restore cultural assets and sacred sites to ensure the recognition and honoring of our collective struggles and triumphs.[11]

Their reparation demands also point out that Chicago passed legislation providing "free city college tuition and job training to victims [of police torture], their immediate family members and their grandchildren; and funded psychological, family, substance abuse, and other counseling services to victims and their immediate family members."

You can see how Black LIES Matter is now just a propaganda and get-out-the-vote arm of the Democratic Party. I know the Democratic

Party did not found the group, but don't you know those political "leaders" are looking at this as an opportunity to enrage and energize black people to come out and vote. Their ultimate goal is to try to extract perks from the government that they haven't earned. They want political power, money, and other coddling by the nanny state, and they're trying to do it by force, threats, rioting, and other tawdry tactics.

Here's the truth. Black LIES Matters is nothing more than an AstroTurf operation, a shallowly disguised confederation of community organizers and leftists who specialize in fostering rebellion in ghettos and other struggling areas throughout the United States of America.

It doesn't care any more about the lives of black people than the Ku Klux Klan does. Want proof? Turn the page. But only if you have the guts to read the truth.

8

A Hate Group's Battle Cry: #BlackLivesMatter

IN MAY 1999, a fifty-five-year-old black man named Jamil Abdullah Al-Amin was driving a stolen Ford Explorer around the outskirts of Atlanta when he was stopped by police. The officers approached his vehicle, but he flashed a police badge from a small town in Alabama. They let him go but soon realized they'd been had. Because Al-Amin's badge wasn't authentic, he was later indicted on charges of driving without proof of insurance, theft, and impersonating an officer.

When he didn't show up for his court date, two Fulton County sheriff's deputies went to one of Atlanta's poorer neighborhoods to serve him a warrant. It was March 16, 2000. The deputies had been told he was possibly armed, but they had no idea what kind of situation they were approaching.

To start with, Al-Amin was also known as Hubert Gerold Brown. He was a towering, "hawk-faced" man. By the time he started his political activism as chairman of the Student Nonviolent Coordinating Committee (SNCC) in 1967, he went by the name of H. Rap Brown.

When the SNCC merged with the Black Panthers, he was appointed their "minister of justice."

"Violence is as American as cherry pie," he proclaimed. And "if America don't come around, we're gonna burn it down." He wrote a memoir titled *Die, N—, Die!*[1] in which he expressed his views on this nation. (I'll save you the money so you don't have to buy the book; they weren't favorable.) Soon, he made a speech in Maryland, urging black people to get guns and be "ready to die" and to use violence to further their political goals. "This town is ready to explode . . . if you don't have guns, don't be here," he said. "You have to be prepared to die."

In the least surprising development of all time, his listeners were involved in shootings, the destruction of two city blocks, and the destruction of a school.[2] Brown was arrested for inciting a riot. After avoiding trial and carrying a gun across state lines, he became one of the FBI's Ten Most Wanted.

Sounds like a stand-up guy, right?

Originally, his trial was supposed to be held in Cambridge, Maryland, but it was moved to the town of Bel Air at the last minute. On March 9, 1970, two SNCC officials were on US Route 1 south of Bel Air when a bomb exploded, dismembering and killing both of them. Was that bomb an assassination attempt? Or was Brown's group carrying it to be detonated at the courthouse during his trial? The next night the Cambridge courthouse was bombed.

For the next year and a half, Brown lay low. In 1971, however, he was arrested during an attempted robbery of a bar in New York. He spent five years in Attica, where he converted to Islam and changed his name to Jamil Abdullah Al-Amin.

After he got out of prison, he moved to Atlanta. There, he established and became the spiritual leader of a neighborhood mosque and married two women simultaneously. (I say "women," but one of them was in her teens when he married her.) Al-Amin juggled life with two wives—who lived three miles apart from each other—and obligations at a small grocery store he owned and operated.

That's exactly where Fulton County Sheriff's Deputy Ricky Kinchen and fellow Deputy Aldranon English were headed to deliver their warrant, though they had no idea they were pursuing such a violent black nationalist. It just so happened that both Deputy English and Deputy Kinchen were black as well. Deputy Kinchen had received his degree from the historically black Morris Brown College and had been an officer for nine years. He was married to Sherese, with whom he had two kids.

When the officers approached the grocery store, things went bad fast. That's what the public doesn't really understand about police work. One moment, you are doing a routine task. The next you're fighting for your life. Al-Amin shot at the officers with a .223 rifle. Deputy English was wounded immediately and stumbled to a nearby field for cover. Deputy Kinchen tried to protect his partner, but was shot and dropped to the ground. When Al-Amin ran out of ammunition, he went to his black Mercedes and got out a 9mm pistol. He walked back to Deputy Kinchen who was lying on the ground dying. He pointed the gun at the officer and shot him—one, two, three times—right between the legs.

The deputy did not survive the attack.

When Deputy Kinchen was buried, the line of police cruisers— lights flashing—stretched for miles outside the church. Thousands of public servants (firefighters, police officers, and transportation officers) drove from across Georgia to pay their respects in a service that lasted four hours. The Fulton County sheriff gave Sherese her husband's badge, telling her they would retire his number. The service ended when his flag-draped casket was carried slowly to a hearse while the honor guard stood at attention and a lone bagpipe played "Amazing Grace."[3]

"I wipe my tears and stay strong for my children because I know that they are hurting too," his widow said at the trial.[4] There, Deputy District Attorney Ron E. Dixon described Al-Amin as "buck-naked guilty." He urged the jury of two whites, nine blacks, and one Hispanic to impose the maximum penalty. He pointed out Al-Amin's brutality in shooting the officer in the groin. Ultimately, they agreed.

On March 13, 2002, Al-Amin was convicted of murder. Life in prison. No parole.

Justice had been served, and Deputy Kinchen was honored as the hero he was.

On May 2, 1973, Joanne Deborah Chesimard and two friends were driving down the New Jersey Turnpike about an hour south of New York City. Chesimard was in the passenger seat when the vehicle was pulled over for a routine traffic stop. It would be no average traffic stop. Chesimard, who'd changed her name to Assata Shakur, was already on the run after being wanted for several felonies in New York, including bank robbery. Even though she was only twenty-six at the time, she was a leader of the Black Liberation Army, one of the most militant and violent organizations of the 1970s. She'd also been a Black Panther.

New Jersey state troopers James Harper and Werner Foerster had flagged the vehicle down for a broken taillight. But when they approached the vehicle, Shakur pulled out a semiautomatic pistol and fired a shot. The passenger in the back seat fired multiple shots at the officers as well, but Trooper Harper killed him. The driver got out of the car and engaged in hand-to-hand combat with Trooper Foerster, while Shakur began shooting at both officers.

A bullet hit Trooper Foerster in the abdomen and arm, and he fell down along the side of the turnpike. That's when, according to police reports, Shakur picked up the officer's gun and shot him execution-style. *Bam! Bam!* Two shots right in the head. The officer was only thirty-four years old.

The three ran, but state police caught Shakur about half an hour after the shooting. One accomplice's body was found near their abandoned car; the other was arrested about forty hours later.

Shakur was sentenced to life in prison (plus another sixty-five years for murder and assault), but she had other plans. Six years after the incident, three members of the Black Liberation Army visited the prison. When they got in, they pulled out their concealed .45-caliber pistols, pointed them at the guards' heads, took two guards hostage, and drove a stolen prison van right through an unfenced section of the minimum-security facility.

In 1984, Shakur managed to get to Cuba, where she was granted political asylum, and the government there gave her money for living expenses. She has called herself a "20th-century escaped slave" and has written two books in exile.

In 1971, Atlanta police officer Jim Greene pulled his police van into a closed gas station to take a break from patrolling. Two black men approached him. One of them, Freddie Hilton, pretended to ask directions, while the other, Twyman Meyers, approached the passenger window and shot Greene several times.

After shooting the officer, they stole his service weapon and badge. Trophies.

Let's say it together now: Hilton and Meyers were associated with the Black Liberation Army. In Atlanta to learn urban guerrilla tactics, they had become upset when a Black Liberation Army leader berated them for doing "stupid things."[5]

"We did it! We did it!" they exclaimed back at the safe house while showing the officer's gun and badge.[6]

For a long time, no one really paid for this crime. Meyers was killed in a Bronx shootout on November 14, 1973, but Hilton changed his identity and evaded authorities for twenty years. Finally, in 2001, a woman accused her boyfriend of molesting her twelve-year-old daughter. That's when Hilton was arrested in New York. By that time, he was going by Sadiki Kamau and working at the telephone company.

Thanks to the dogged work by a Brooklyn detective, the NYPD was able to connect Hilton to the Greene shooting. The Atlanta cold case detectives were able to get enough evidence while Hilton was doing time in New York to convict him in 2003 of murder. He was also sentenced to life in prison.

Justice had been served.

In 1971 two New York City police officers, twenty-eight-year-old Joseph Piagentini and thirty-four-year-old Waverly Jones, were on foot patrol working to protect the citizens of Harlem in the 32nd Precinct when a call came in: help was needed at the Colonial Park Houses public housing development.

Jones and Piagentini, both of whom were married and had two children, did what police officers all over the nation do every day: they went to help people in need. But it was a bogus call made by Black Liberation Army members Herman Bell, Jalil Abdul Muntaqim (born Anthony Bottom), and Albert "Nuh" Washington, who were hiding and waiting for officers in a staircase of the Macombs Dam Bridge.

It was about 10:00 p.m. As the officers were returning to their patrol car, they were ambushed. Officer Jones, who was black, received four shots to the back of his head and died immediately. Officer Piagentini fell to the sidewalk, bleeding profusely from his wounds. He begged for his life and explained that he had two young daughters he didn't want to be orphaned. The murderers took the revolvers from both police officers and fired every single round into the young man. He died en route to the hospital, having been shot thirteen times.

Office Jones's weapon was later found in San Francisco after several Black Liberation Army members opened fire on a San Francisco police officer.

Bottom was convicted on two counts of first-degree murder and was sentenced to twenty-five years to life. Bell also received twenty-five years to life. Both admitted their involvement in the murders.[7] Washington died in prison.

The FBI's Most Wanted

I've told you these stories *not* to showcase the inherent risks of police work. Not at all. I'm telling you these stories because I want you to get rid of your notion that Black LIES Matter is the type of organization you can get behind. After all, you are black or you have black friends. You love everyone. Why wouldn't you back Black LIES Matter?

The reason will chill you to the bone.

The *New York Times* reported that Movement for Black Lives (a collection of fifty Black Lives Matter groups) released a list of demands "aimed at furthering their goals as the presidential campaign heads into the homestretch." As part of their demands, which I addressed briefly in the previous chapter, they called for the release of "political prisoners" and the removal of "legitimate freedom fighters" from the FBI's Most Wanted Lists.

Who was on that list? The same people from the stories I told:

- **H. Rap Brown**, the man who shot Fulton County Sheriff's Deputy Kinchen and Deputy English when they were delivering his warrant. The one who retrieved his gun from the car to put three bullets between Deputy Kinchen's legs as he lay dying.
- **Assata Shakur**, who shot and killed Trooper Foerster after he pulled her over in a traffic stop. Execution-style. Two shots right in the head.
- **Freddie Hilton**, who pretended to ask directions while his buddy shot Officer Greene to prove he wasn't stupid.
- **Herman Bell** and **Jalil Muntaqim**, who called for help in Harlem because they knew police would respond, and they could ambush them with bullets to the backs of their heads.

Anarchy, the Real Goal

Why would Black LIES Matter want these people free? Especially since several of them murdered black police officers? Because they do not care about black lives. They care about their own radical ideology of terrorism: anarchy. This paints the July 2016 shooting that broke out at a Black LIES Matter rally in Dallas in a totally different light, doesn't it?

You'll remember that the protest was a demonstration against illegal and unfair killings at the hands of police officers. But guess what? They needed cops in order to properly protest, and the Dallas police officers put on their uniforms and stood among the crowds of people who were maligning them. That's what cops do, after all. It's our duty and our honor.

Then, horribly, it turned into bloodshed. A heavily armed sniper began shooting at police officers, picking them off one by one. A dozen police officers returned fire during a series of gun battles that stretched over blocks. The attack, which was carried live on national television, caused Americans to wait with bated breath as the gunman holed up in a parking garage. He was able to hold off the police by falsely stating that he planted bombs in the area. Eventually, a remote-controlled robot delivered an explosive device that killed the sniper. By the end of the night, five officers were dead while seven officers and two civilians were wounded.

As *National Review* pointed out after the shooting, it was not an isolated incident, nor is it new. In the five days surrounding the Dallas shooting—which was the worst police massacre since 9/11, by the way—there was even more Black LIES Matter–inspired violence:[8]

- In Tennessee, a black man who claimed to be motivated by "police violence against African Americans" opened fire on a highway, killing a woman and injuring three others—including a police officer.
- In Missouri, a black motorist ambushed a white police officer after a traffic stop—shooting the officer in the neck and leaving him "fighting for his life."
- Also in Missouri, a young black man threw a planter through the front door of an off-duty police officer's home and advanced into the house while the officer's wife, mother-in-law, and young children tried to escape through a back window. The officer opened fire and killed the intruder. He apparently targeted the home after an online argument over Black Lives Matter.
- In Minnesota, Black Lives Matter protestors attacked police with "rocks, bottles, and other items," injuring twenty-one—including an officer who suffered a broken vertebra "after a concrete block was dropped on his head."

Let me guess. You'd never heard of these incidents. That's because the media protect and lie about this insidious terror organization. And killings keep happening like clockwork. In Baton Rouge on July 17, 2016, days after the Dallas shootings, a man ambushed and killed three law enforcement officers and wounded three others.

When Life Gives You Lemon . . .

All of this happened right after I received an interesting voice mail from Donald Trump Jr., whom I'd met at the NRA Convention a couple of years earlier.

"Hey, I was on a flight with my father today, and we talked about you," Don said when I called him back. His father, of course, was only the Republican nominee for president at the time. He hadn't yet gob-smacked the political world by finally ridding America of the Clinton political machine. "Want to get involved in the GOP Convention?"

"Well, I'll probably be there," I said. "What do you have in mind?"

"We'd like for you to speak," he said.

I didn't want to do that. I want to be a foot soldier promoting conservatism. I didn't need the bright lights and the cameras on me. "That's okay," I said. "I'll be there, but I don't want to do that."

"Sheriff, we really think you ought to do this."

That's when I understood. It was going to be a law and order theme, and they really wanted me on that stage.

"All right," I relented. I packed my bags and headed to Cleveland, along with every media outlet covering the hotly contested race.

The interview requests came pouring in. CNN's Don Lemon asked me to do his show on location from the RNC. Lemon, a black news anchor who voted for Barack Obama twice, has been described as one of the "fastest-rising stars" and "one of the worst reporters of 2014."[9] I was about to see at least half of that.

First of all, it's very hard to get into media row at these events. If you don't have the passes, you aren't getting in. CNN was supposed to have people meet me to get me past the guard, but they didn't show up. Finally, a CNN field reporter overheard me talking to the guards and got my wife, Julie, my friend, and me through. While we were walking up, two interns approached me. By this time, it was getting late. I'd been up since 6:00 a.m. doing media. I hadn't had time to eat dinner, so I felt like a little courtesy was due. I was pretty hot, to say the least.

"Sheriff Clarke, we're so sorry."

"I'm doing you guys a favor," I said. "I didn't ask to be on this show."

"Yes, we're sorry."

"Apologies are for funerals. They don't work in business," I said. "You guys run a Mickey Mouse operation here."

Eventually, we made it to the booth. I was supposed to be on the air soon, but I waited and waited as I watched Lemon take a guest, then another, then another.

I went up to the scheduler and tapped on my watch. "What happened?"

"Oh, you'll be up soon."

"My watch has numbers on it," I said calmly. "And none of them say 'soon.'"

When they finally got me on, I was fit to be tied.

"Hello, Sheriff Clarke," Lemon said when I sat down. "How are you?"

"I've been better," I said. I think he sensed that this interview was going to be like none other.

I don't get emotional frequently, but I do when I hear of police deaths. I will not let others get away with platitudes. I knew that Black Lives Matter movement is an anarchist movement that runs parallel with the violence of the 1960s, but it's been masked and wrapped around poor blacks. They put that on as a mask to gain support and sympathy from the unsuspecting public who might be watching from afar, reading about it in a newspaper or watching it on TV. Years ago, I decided I was going to unmask them, but Lemon apparently didn't get the memo. Things went bad from the very first moments of Lemon's show after he began by saying he spoke to the Baton Rouge sheriff's department and police department.

"Their message is peace and coming together in the country. What's your message?"

"You don't believe that for one minute, do you?" I asked. I knew his game. CNN has implicitly endorsed the Black LIES Matter movement by framing the organization as sensitive to black matters, and I wasn't going to let them flaunt their sensitivity in front of me. I wasn't going to let them pander.

Lemon was at a loss for words—a first. "Uh, that's what they said to me," he managed to say after a few seconds of dead air. "Yeah, I believe them."

"Any protests over the deaths of these cops today in Baton Rouge?" I asked. I was trying to tell Lemon he didn't want to get into the ring with me.

"I don't know."

"Any riots or protests over the officers in Dallas, Texas?"

"What are you asking?"

"It's a pretty simple question," I said. "My message has been clear from day one, two years ago. This anticop sentiment from this hateful ideology called Black Lives Matter has fueled this rage against the American police officer. I predicted this two years ago."

"Okay, Sheriff. With all due respect," he said (you know it's never good when a sentence begins with that phrase), "do you know that this was because of that? As a law enforcement officer?"

"I've been watching this for two years. I predicted this," I said. "This antipolice rhetoric sweeping the country has turned out some hateful things inside of people that are now playing themselves out on the American police officer. I want to know, with all of the black-on-black violence in the United States of America . . . By the way, when the tragedies happened in Louisiana and Minnesota, do you know that twenty-one black people were murdered across the United States? Was there any reporting on that?"

"Let's keep the volume down," he said to me as if he was my preschool teacher.

"I'm looking at three dead cops this week and five last week," I said, incredulous. "You're trying to tell me to keep it down?"

At one, point, exasperated, Lemon said, "I feel like we're having two different conversations." I think that may have been the only accurate thing he uttered during our very awkward nine-minute interview. We have one conversation that the media are hosting, and the other that America knows to be true. "I'm trying to keep it civil," Lemon said. "I'm sure the message you want to convey to people at home is one of civility."

He went on to argue that black-on-black violence was a "separate topic" that didn't pertain to the Black LIES Matter shootings. In other words, he wanted to push the narrative that Black Lives Matter is about racial equality, and I wanted to show him that it's an antipolice hate group based on the lie of police brutality. I wasn't backing down.

"Don, I wish *you* had that message of civility," I said. But when I began to elaborate on my point—that Black LIES Matter is a hate group—he went to a commercial break.

That must've given him time to think because after the commercial break, he tried to pull one over on me. "Sheriff Clarke, we can't sit here and talk over each other. If you think that I don't care about these eight dead cops, then you can leave right now."

I knew that trick. Lemon wanted me to rip off the microphone, storm off the set, and make a big scene. I thought, *I'm too smart for that. I'm not going anywhere. You can go to another commercial break, but I'm not going anywhere.* Had I fallen for his suggestion, the headlines would've been "Sheriff Clarke storms off CNN." That's why I stuck around until the end.

When the segment was finally over, I walked off the set and received the stony glare of the producer. If looks could kill, I would've been a dead man.

My friend Craig and my wife, Julie, were at the studio with me, but they couldn't hear the words that were being said. Don and I were in an enclosed booth behind glass, so they had only watched the screens, none of which had volume.

"Let's get out of here," I said to Julie and Craig.

"How did it go?" Julie asked, looking concerned.

"What was going on in there?" Craig said. "You got pretty animated."

"Let's just hope that thing goes viral," I said.

Sure enough, it did. Millions of people saw the video on the Internet, and it turned out that everyone was happy I didn't let CNN get away with pandering to blacks. Remember how Barack Obama said that America needs to have a conversation about race? Well, no one really wants that conversation. It's hard, it's uncomfortable, and it gets people riled up. They don't want to have a dialogue. They want people like me to sit down and shut up.

Don Lemon found out that I, for one, am not going to play by their rules. That's why Trump wanted me to speak at the convention, and I was more motivated and honored than ever to stand before an enormous national audience and speak truth about the importance of supporting first responders and making America safe again.

Every convention speaker gets time with a speaking coach. I thought they might help write the speech for me, but the Trump people wanted this to be 100 percent me. They gave me the strict parameters of a five-minute speech, but I got it down only to about eight. Though I'd planned on shortening it, I was so busy I never got around to editing it. Plus, it was the right length. I'd pared it down to precisely what I wanted to say.

When I met with my speech coach and he heard my rehearsal, he said, "You're a natural. You're going to knock this out of the park." He did give me two pieces of great advice: "Number one, walk to the podium as if you have something important to say and you can't wait to say it. Number two, don't try to speak over the applause. It doesn't work, slows the momentum, and sounds stilted."

And so, when the moment arrived, I strode out to the podium with a purpose. "Ladies and gentlemen, I would like to make something very clear," I said. "Blue Lives Matter in America!" The crowd went nuts. Later I realized that this was the loudest and longest applause that any speaker had received that week. I was profoundly sobered by this opportunity. Many VIPs were at the convention, but the Trump campaign gave me, the Milwaukee County sheriff, a prime-time slot. Since I was told not to speak over the applause, the cheering of the crowd gave me time to collect myself. I make speeches all the time, but this was the biggest moment of my life. Twenty thousand people were in the arena, but millions were watching from home. As the crowd cheered, I took a breath.

I stand before you tonight with a heavy heart as the law enforcement community prepares to bury three of Baton Rouge,

Louisiana's, finest. But there is some good news out of Baltimore, Maryland, as Lt. Brian Rice was acquitted on all charges, and the malicious prosecution of activist State's Attorney Marilyn Mosby.

The crowd booed when I mentioned Mosby's name, so I paused again.

I want to talk to you about something important, indeed, a concept that five law enforcement officers were murdered and nine more were wounded for, earlier this month, and for which three more were murdered two days ago in Baton Rouge, Louisiana: And that is the importance of making America safe again. You see, I believe that this noble mission is not just a requirement, but a prerequisite for achieving this campaign's goal of making America great again. We simply cannot be great if we do not feel safe in our homes, on our streets, and in our schools.

When I do speeches or interviews on television, I hope to find "the zone." When I get into that zone, I'm pretty oblivious to a lot of this.

Afterward, people came up to me and said, "That was the best speech!"

I had to take their word for it. I didn't remember saying any of it. The words were just coming out—coherent and powerful—but I didn't hear myself delivering it. It was almost as if I didn't get to experience my RNC speech until I saw it on television later. It was a great privilege to be able to speak at the RNC. But it was an even bigger *honor* to show respect and support to my fellow officers around the country, to open America's eyes to the motives and hate behind Black LIES Matter.

9

The Second Amendment
Isn't Just for White People

LET ME SHARE A SECRET.

I've had the privilege of going around this nation and speaking to God-fearing Americans. I've had the honor of meeting some of you, hearing your stories, and sharing at least a part of your lives. Frequently, people ask the same question: "Why do I salute the audience when I speak?"

I'm old school. In our representative democracy, elected officials are not sovereign. You the people are sovereign. In keeping with military custom, it is incumbent on the subordinate officer to salute and render that salute first to the superior officer. I consider myself the subordinate officer. That's why I salute my audience because they're in charge, not the political class. This is American Government 101, but this attitude is far too rare in modern society.

I think that's why people are surprised when they see me salute at the beginning of my speeches about race, police, crime, the Constitution, rule of law, and the Second Amendment. They are used to elected officials condescending to them, which is exactly the opposite way America is supposed to work. I salute to honor them and to remind them of the proper order of things. Guess what? I've learned a few things as well. After all of my speeches in so many places across this nation, no topic causes as much emotion, passion, or vilification as the subject of guns.

Backlash Against My PSAs

Why do academia, the liberal media, and liberals in the political establishment treat the Second Amendment like the illegitimate child of the Bill of Rights? I learned the answer to this question the hard way when I made a series of public service announcements in 2013.

"I'm Sheriff David Clarke, and I want to talk to you about something personal . . . your safety," I said into the recorder in my office. I had no idea I was about to strike a chord that would reverberate through the culture and cause NPR to describe my baritone voice as "ominous." It was January, and the budget for my office had been cut drastically. It was time to get real with the residents of Milwaukee County. I began the first announcement with these words:

> Your safety is no longer a spectator sport; I need you in the game, but are you ready? With officers laid off and furloughed, simply calling 911 and waiting is no longer your best option. You can beg for mercy from a violent criminal, hide under the bed, or you can fight back; but are you prepared? Consider taking a certified safety course in handling a firearm so you can defend yourself until we get there. You have a duty to protect yourself and your family. We're partners now. Can I count on you?

My second ad had a similar theme:

This is Sheriff David Clarke. Violent crime went up nearly 10 percent in Milwaukee. Are you the next victim? You don't have to be! But that's your call. Armed criminals are being put back on the street by a soft-on-crime court system even before the ink dries on police reports. Are you prepared to handle a life-or-death threat? Wisconsin's Personal Protection Act now gives you the same advantage that I have. Now it's the crook who has to wonder what you might do. It can be a great equalizer . . . but you always have to think survival . . . Remember, it's you and me now.

And the third was about refusing to be victimized, and it also struck a chord that liberals hated:

I'm Sheriff Clarke. To avoid being a victim of crime you don't have to be the toughest or fastest person on the block. Your age and gender don't matter either. Here's what's important . . . attention to your surroundings is critical . . . recognize the threat . . . know who's around you when walking down the street, getting into your car, or going into your home. And if you smell trouble? Trust your instincts . . . be decisive . . . use the element of surprise against your attacker, and most importantly, be ruthless in your response. Are you ready?

These ads sparked much conversation across Milwaukee and beyond to the rest of the nation. Mayor Tom Barrett said, "Apparently Sheriff David Clark [sic] is auditioning for the next Dirty Harry movie." County Executive Chris Abele said, "I think it's irresponsible, and it doesn't help public safety to tell the public there's some kind of imminent danger that they need to go buy guns. Essentially, you've got a [public service announcement] that's recommending people need to go buy guns because they can't rely on the response they'll get from 911. I'm here to tell you, we have phenomenal police departments." Jeri Bonavia, of the nonprofit Wisconsin Anti-violence Effort, said, "If he does not feel he is capable of doing this [protecting Milwaukee citizens], and he's not qualified to take on this role of public safety, he should resign and he should do it today. To issue a blanket statement that people should be out there, arming up, and taking care of safety matters that really law enforcement officials are trained to do, is just irresponsible."[1]

In other words, because of my little public service announcements, I was accused of vigilantism, fear mongering, misinformation, and incompetence. (But I have to point out to Mayor Barrett that the Dirty Harry movies were about Inspector Harry Callahan of the San Francisco Police Department using excessive force to combat bad guys, not about promoting true self-defense. Plus, I think the likelihood of you actually having seen even one Dirty Harry movie is about as strong as you having read the Constitution.) The real reason the radio ad was controversial was that people have so many misconceptions about police, guns, history, and even minorities.

Let me explain this common misconception about police: we cannot protect you, at least not all of you all of the time. In 2005, the Supreme Court of the United States ruled that police do not have a constitutional obligation to protect someone, no matter what the mottos say on the police car doors.[2] In a country with 325 million people, citizens can never abdicate responsibility for their own family's personal safety to anyone else—even the police.[3] Why?

Criminologist and professor Don B. Kates Jr. explained the numbers:

Even if all 500,000 American police officers were assigned to patrol, they could not protect 240 million citizens from upwards of 10 million criminals who enjoy the luxury of deciding when and where to strike. But we have nothing like 500,000 patrol officers; to determine how many police are actually available for any one shift, we must divide the 500,000 by four (three shifts per day, plus officers who have days off, are on sick leave, etc.). The resulting number must be cut in half to account for officers assigned to investigations, juvenile, records, laboratory, traffic, etc., rather than patrol.[4]

In other words, there simply are not enough of us to protect all of you. Once the wolf is at the door, once the intruder is inside your home, once you're on the street and someone sticks a gun in your face to take your car or your wallet, you don't have the option of calling 911.

You've heard the old saying: when seconds count, the police are minutes away. That's not a slam on police. You don't want to live under martial law where cops are on every corner. People, it's called "self-defense" for a reason. You must take charge of *yourself*. One reason why self-defense has gone out of fashion is that we have forgotten how much of history—even the Bible—emphasizes its importance.

Historical Take on Self-Defense

The founders of our country knew this. In his first address to both houses of Congress, George Washington said, "A free people ought not only to be armed, but disciplined; to which end a uniform and well-digested plan is requisite; and their safety and interest require that they should promote such manufactories as tend to render them independent of others for essential, particularly military, supplies." In the 1788 debates of the Massachusetts Convention, Samuel Adams said that the Constitution should never be interpreted "to authorize Congress to . . . prevent the people of the United States, who are peaceable citizens, from keeping their own arms."[5]

Thomas Jefferson advised, "Let your gun therefore be your constant companion of your walks."[6] Even more to the point, he wrote, "The constitutions of most of our States [and of the United States] assert, that all power is inherent in the people; that they may exercise it by themselves, in all cases to which they think themselves competent . . . ; that it is their right and duty to be at all times armed."[7]

Did you catch that? It's your *right* and your *duty*. When I uttered in my radio ad that "you have a duty to protect yourself and your family," Anti-Gun-Idiots (AGIs) went nuts. But it's hardly a radical statement. It's what Americans have believed all along. Humanity has believed this for thousands of years. Even a cursory reading of the Bible shows the necessity of preserving life—of yourself and others. For example, in 1 Corinthians 6:19–20 (KJV), the author wrote, "Know ye not that your body is the temple of the Holy Ghost which is in you, which ye have of God, and ye are not your own? For ye are bought with a price: therefore glorify God in your body."

This is why I get up every day committed to an exercise regimen. But not only are we to be physically healthy; we are to protect those who are more vulnerable. The Bible speaks to that throughout, but here are two verses that jump out at me.

Rescue the weak and the needy; deliver them from the hand of the wicked. (Psalm 82:4 NIV)

Deliver those who are drawn toward death, and hold back those stumbling to the slaughter. (Proverbs 24:11 NKJV)

And the Bible even stipulates we have a moral obligation to warn people of possible danger:

If the watchman sees the sword coming and does not blow the trumpet, and the people are not warned, and a sword comes and takes a person from them, he is taken away in his iniquity; but his blood I will require from the watchman's hand. (Ezekiel 33:6 NASB)

Though it's our obligation to warn of the attack, people have to figure out their own response. Later, the Scriptures explain that if people don't heed the watchman's warnings, that's on them. Furthermore, we need to maintain and control our property to make sure our friends and family are safe from injury. Exodus 21:29 warns that if a man is so careless that his bull kills someone, the owner should be put to death. Deuteronomy 22:8 tells people to make sure they build their homes in such a way to prevent anyone from falling off the roof.

You can't put it any more plainly: we are responsible for our own lives and for others. Proverbs 25:26 (NKJV) instructs that "a righteous man who falters before the wicked is like a murky spring and a polluted well." If a bad guy tries to injure you or your family, that is not the time to be caught off guard, without training, without the proper weapons. First Timothy 5:8 (NKJV) states, "If anyone does not provide for his own, and especially for those of his household, he has denied the faith and is worse than an unbeliever."

So, how do you provide for yourself and your family? Among other things, by protecting them. Jesus instructed his disciples to carry a weapon. Luke 22:35–36 records a conversation he and his friends were having before going to a prayer meeting: "He said to them, 'When I sent you without money bag, knapsack, and sandals, did you lack anything?' So they said, 'Nothing.' Then He said to them, 'But now, he who has a money bag, let him take it, and likewise a knapsack; and he who has no sword, let him sell his garment and buy one'" (NKJV).

His disciples, however, pointed out they were already armed: "So they said, 'Lord, look, here are two swords.' And He said to them, 'It is enough'" (Luke 22:38 NKJV). Imagine that conversation. If that were to happen today, his friends would've pulled back their jackets, pointed to their holsters, and said, "We're already carrying. Are two Glocks enough, or do we need more?"

Isn't it interesting that the friends of Jesus carried personal weapons? Not only did he know about their weapons, he advised them on how much protection was necessary, actually encouraging them to be armed. Carrying weapons for self-defense has always been a part of American history and a part of our Judeo-Christian heritage. So why did everyone become apoplectic over my radio ads?

I have to believe that some of the uproar had to do with the fact that I am black and I was speaking to an audience that was at least partially comprised of blacks. America has mixed-up messages when it comes to black people and guns. But I have news for you, Anti-Gun-Idiots: the Second Amendment isn't just for white people anymore.

Guns and Black People

America has a long and complicated history regarding guns and black people. At first, the colonial settlers did everything they could to make sure black people and Native Americans didn't get their hands on weapons. Massachusetts and Plymouth colonists couldn't legally sell guns to Native Americans, while black Virginia and Tennessee residents couldn't own guns even if they were free. In 1857, the chief justice of the United States, Roger B. Taney, explained why the Supreme Court couldn't possibly grant Dred Scott's petition in the famous court case.

Dred Scott was a slave "owned" by an army doctor who had lived in one free state and one free territory—Illinois and Wisconsin. The case dealt with one important question: Should slavery be allowed in the West? The court, stacked with pro-slavery justices, affirmed the right of owners to take their slaves west. Scott would not be free, they decided, because he was considered merely property.

"It would give to persons of the negro race," Chief Justice Roger B. Taney wrote in the majority decision ". . . the right to enter every other State whenever they pleased . . . to sojourn there as long as they pleased, to go where they pleased . . . the full liberty of speech in public and in private upon all subjects upon which its own citizens might speak; to hold public meetings upon political affairs, and to keep and carry arms wherever they went."

Black people crossing state lines? Speaking their minds? With guns? Pass the smelling salts! But his opinion showed how much slavery equals government tyranny. The government knows all too well that the first step to enslave people is to disarm them, and the first step to liberate them is to arm them.

You know the rest of the story. Eventually blacks were given citizenship, but the Thirteenth Amendment freed the slaves only on paper. Even after the Civil War, some southern states enacted Black Codes that prohibited blacks from owning guns. In 1866, Congress overrode most portions of these codes by passing the Civil Rights Act; the Fourteenth Amendment passed two years later. States, however, still used taxes and high costs to keep black people and poor whites from owning guns. Virginia's official university law review suggested a "prohibitive tax . . . on the privilege" of the sale of weapons to prevent "the son of Ham" from getting them. After all, the statement said, black people's "cowardly practice of 'toting' guns has been one of the most fruitful sources of crime . . . Let a negro board a railroad train with a quart of mean whiskey and a pistol in his grip and the chances are that there will be a murder, or at least a row, before he alights."[8] Frequently, only certain types of guns would be available to purchase—the kinds that only whites already had or could easily afford.

But early civil rights activist Ida B. Wells, in her argument against southern lynching, wrote that guns were the best deterrent against assault. "The only times an Afro-American who was assaulted got away has been when he had a gun and used it in self-defense." Black people embraced gun ownership as their God-given right to showcase—and, in some cases, guarantee—their freedom. In modern America, regrettably, that has not been the case, and it might have to do with a simplistic understanding of the civil rights movement.

The Civil Rights Movement

When you think about the civil rights movement, the first people who come to mind are nonviolent protestors who rightfully went down in history for their remarkable courage and fortitude. Martin Luther King Jr. wrote in his first book, *Stride Toward Freedom*, that nonviolent resistance is "a courageous confrontation of evil by the power of love."[9] He wrote that "the Christian doctrine of love operating through the Gandhian method of nonviolence was one of the most potent weapons available to oppressed people in their struggle for freedom."

Rosa Parks famously refused to surrender her seat to a white man on a Montgomery, Alabama, bus. Instead of violently protesting the injustice, she organized a boycott to end the segregation. The boycott forced the city to change the law requiring segregation, which earned Parks the NAACP's highest award and the nickname "the first lady of civil rights."

These stories of the brave men and women paved the way for a nation full of the liberty and opportunity I enjoy. However, I think the emphasis on the civil rights nonviolent protest strategy often over-shadows the more complicated truth about how blacks and guns do (and should) interact; it has separated blacks from their history.

For example, did you know that even people like these stalwarts of the nonviolent civil rights protests believed robustly in self-defense? Though he was denied a carry permit, King had what was described as a "veritable arsenal at home" to defend his family.

Frederick Douglass escaped slavery and became the great abolition-ist orator still revered to this day. In 1850, he was asked what was the best response to the Fugitive Slave Act, which harshly penalized anyone for interfering in the capture and return of runaway slaves. Douglass responded simply, "A good revolver."[10]

Wells, the activist who wrote so powerfully against southern lynch-ing, offered good advice: "A Winchester rifle should have a place of honor in every black home, and it should be used for that protection which the law refuses to give."

This desire to take charge of their own safety wasn't unusual. "Far from being a digression from the principle of nonviolence," Charles C. W. Cooke wrote in the *New York Times*, "this willingness to defend oneself was heir to a long, proud tradition."

What people don't get—and what liberals want us to forget—is that there's a qualitative difference between violence and self-defense, even if the acts look the same. Imagine this scenario. A thief walks into a home, grabs a knife from a drawer, and slits the throat of an unsuspecting woman while she cooks. Now imagine another scenario. A woman is cooking when she sees a thief come into the kitchen. As he lunges toward her to attack her, she grabs a knife from the drawer and slits his throat.

These two scenarios look very similar—in one, a man slits a woman's throat; in the other a woman slits a man's throat. The first is cold-blooded murder. The second is self-defense. Every civilization throughout history has made a distinction that one is perfectly unacceptable and the other is perfectly acceptable.

Even Gandhi, on whose principles King based his philosophies, believed in self-defense. "I do believe that where there is only a choice between cowardice and violence I would advise violence," he wrote in his book *Doctrine of the Sword*. He came to this realization the hard way. In 1908, he was assaulted and almost killed. He described the attack afterward by writing,

> I took severe blows on my left ribs. Even now I find breathing difficult. My upper lip has a cut on one side. I have a bruise above the left eye and a wound on the forehead. In addition, there are minor injuries on my right hand and left knee. I do not remember the manner of the assault, but people say that I fell down unconscious with the first blow which was delivered with a stick. Then my assailants struck me with an iron pipe and a stick, and they also kicked me. Thinking me dead, they stopped. I only remember having been beaten up. I have an impression that, as the blows started, I uttered the words "He Rama!" [Oh God] . . . As I came to, I got up with a smile. In my mind there was not the slightest anger or hatred for the assailants.[11]

Interestingly, he reported that he had no feelings of ill will toward his attackers. But even though he didn't blame them, he had interesting advice for his son: "When my eldest son asked me what he should have done, had he been present when I was almost fatally assaulted in 1908, whether he should have run away and seen me killed or whether he should have used his physical force which he could and wanted to use, and defended me, I told him that it was his duty to defend me even by using violence."

I'd push it even further. Malcolm X rightly said, "I don't even call it violence when it's in self-defense; I call it intelligence." As Cooke wrote, "Malcolm X may have a deservedly mixed reputation, but the famous photograph of him standing at the window, rifle in hand, insisting on black liberation 'by any means necessary,' is about as American as it gets. It should be celebrated just like the 'Don't tread on me' Gadsden flag."

He's right. Though blacks should be strong defenders of the Second Amendment and gun rights, the antigun Left has hoodwinked us to be antigun. Although most gun owners are God-fearing, freedom-loving patriots who support the US Constitution, President Obama maligned them by calling them "bitter clingers." He said that when things don't go right, we cling to our guns and our religion. (Which is exactly right, federal government, so don't forget it.) They have tried to make their cause less white to garner more sympathy from an unsuspecting general public.

It's worked.

The *Washington Post* conducted a fascinating study on gun ownership that revealed an enormous racial disparity:

Black Americans and white Americans hold divergent attitudes about gun ownership. About 41 percent of white households own guns, compared to just 19 percent of black households, according to a 2014 Pew survey. And white Americans (62 percent) are more likely than black Americans (54 percent) to say that gun ownership does more to protect people than endanger personal safety. Those different experiences partly explain their divergent views: Whites (61 percent) are nearly twice as likely as blacks (34 percent) to say it's more important to protect gun rights than to control gun ownership.[12]

In other words, this high homicide rate comes from a population with a very low rate of gun ownership. White Americans have more experience with guns and are subjected to less criminal gun violence. That's why you should never buy the argument that more guns equals more violence. It's just not true. White liberal Americans had a problem with my radio ads because they didn't want black Americans defending themselves. The NRA should best be understood as a civil rights group.

"To disarm the people," wrote George Mason, "was the best and most effectual way to enslave them." In 1775, our renegade Founding Fathers, the framers of the Constitution, understood the threat posed by a strong central government. They created self-rule around a document that places the power with the people. They understood government tyranny was a natural result of government, so they created safeguards. They knew that only an armed citizenry can keep government in check. "Arms discourage and keep the invader and plunderer in awe, and preserve order in the world as well as property," Thomas Paine wrote. "Horrid mischief would ensue were the law-abiding deprived of the use of them."

Turns out "horrid mischief" was an understatement. It's a historical truism that in the twentieth century, Nazi Germany's use of firearm registration laws to confiscate weapons from Jews rendered them defenseless from attacks. Switzerland's tradition of men armed with military weapons kept at home ready to organize into a militia of total resistance played a significant role in dissuading Nazi invasion during World War II.

Survival is the first law of nature because human beings have an inherent desire to survive. Sometimes that means fighting off criminal predators.

The people who believe guns should be restricted are stuck on stupid about what causes mass shootings, violence, and suicides. Benjamin Franklin said, "We are all born ignorant, but one must work hard to remain stupid."

When he said that, he had to have this gun-grabbing group in mind. A gun in the hands of a law-abiding citizen is a threat only to the criminal. It is also a threat to an ever-expanding federal government hell-bent on trying to destroy your right to bear arms.

Folks, my ancestors shed blood for the right to bear arms for self-defense. I will not cede that right back to the government.

Neither should you.

10

Changing the Culture
Is a Matter of Faith, Not Politics

A PRIEST WALKED UP TO ME, a smile on his face. "I am Canon Benoît Jayr," he said while warmly shaking my hand. Behind him, I noticed congregants of all ages buzzing around the pews cleaning, polishing, and mending the old church.

I was doing my rounds on the south side of Milwaukee, an area where Polish immigrants made their home during the mid-1800s. They fled their native country in such numbers that they created home-away-from-home on Lincoln Avenue and Mitchell Street, which became dotted with Polish bakeries, grocery stores, taverns, and butcher shops. Polish flats popped up, one story at a time, to save money and to allow room for their ever-growing families. But the center of life for Milwaukee's Polish community was the church. In 1866, the first large Polish church in all of the major American cities was built.

Of course, neighborhoods—especially in Milwaukee—are vibrant and dynamic, changing according to what's going on in the world. In the early 1900s, Mexican immigrants began coming to Milwaukee for the same reason the Poles did: America had more opportunity than their home country. Mexican men worked in Milwaukee's tanneries, hot and dirty places that turned hides into leather, but were still better than the job opportunities in Mexico. Before long, Mexican grocery stores, restaurants, and other businesses started popping up around the area. Now, if you drive down Mitchell Street—once the Polish shopping hub—you can find all kinds of Hispanic businesses. Today, Saint Stanislaus Church, which used to offer masses in the Polish language, offers a Sunday mass in Spanish. (It also offers a mass in Latin, which I love—old school.)

On the day of my visit, to add even more ethnic diversity to the south side equation, a smiling French priest greeted this black sheriff.

"Thank you for protecting this community," Rev. Jayr said, his English perfect but his accent heavy. "In France, we do not have sheriffs. The only way I had heard of 'sheriff' was on American western films. And here you are with your boots and cowboy hat. You look exactly how I imagined a sheriff would look."

I get that a lot. People thank me for "saving the community." However, the truth is that the priest, and others like Rev. Jayr are doing the real work that transforms communities. Faith transforms: sheriffs, policies, entitlement programs, and politicians do not. Some politicians hold faith in such disregard that they do more harm than good.

I'll give you one of the more dramatic examples.

No God in the Platform

In 2012, the Democratic Convention was held in Charlotte, North Carolina, where delegates from all over the nation went to nominate Barack Obama as their incumbent candidate for president of the United States. That year, however, when Democratic leaders drafted their platform, they'd removed all references to Jerusalem as the capital of Israel, even though support for Israel has been a vital part of the

Democratic platform for about six decades. Oh, and they eliminated all references to God.

To be clear, they hadn't forgotten to include these references. They had consciously scrubbed these references from previous platforms. Their actions didn't play well with people outside the Beltway. All over America, commonsense, God-fearing Democrats expressed their anger. Even Harvard Law School's Alan Dershowitz described the Democratic Party as the first major American political party to abandon Israel. The party leaders realized they'd better fix this. They didn't want their nominee (whose religion had already caused much speculation around American watercoolers) to be shackled with also being anti-God. They placed an amendment to the platform on the convention's agenda.

Antonio Villaraigosa, the mayor of Los Angeles, was apparently instructed to pass the platform change regardless of the actual vote. When the amendment went up on the floor, a sizeable number of delegates started yelling, "No!" They didn't want God or Jerusalem in their platform. TV cameras showed close-ups of delegates holding "Palestinians for Obama" signs high above their heads as they screamed against the vote. The votes seemed like a pretty even split, but a platform change requires a two-thirds majority. Mayor Villaraigosa, unable to ignore the dissenting voices, looked confused and shocked. So he asked for a revote. Then another. After the third revote, they still had no consensus. Knowing the Democrats needed God in their platform, Villaraigosa ignored the dissenters and declared the amendment had passed.

Turns out, God's place in the Democratic Party was tenuous at best because after this "victory," the unbelievable happened. The crowd booed God on national television. It was one of those images that you can never unsee. The Democratic Party elites were sending a loud and clear message to America that there is no room for God in their ranks.

It has become a pattern. Four years later, candidate Mrs. Bill Clinton attended a campaign rally in Blackwood, New Jersey. Camden County Board of Freeholders member Susan Shin Angulo introduced her to the crowd. Angulo said that Mrs. Bill Clinton could create a nation "filled with promise and opportunity and not of fear, demagoguery, or radicalism." Then, she added that Clinton could bring us "together, as one nation u-uhh . . . indivisible with liberty and justice for all." The unspoken words—*under God*—hung in the air like a ghost. Clinton laughed and nodded in approval at the omission.

But an antifaith movement is not a new development for the Democratic Party. When Bill Clinton was running against George H. W. Bush, remember how the liberal media and Democrats (oh, but I repeat myself) mocked Dan Quayle for advocating for "family values"?

The Value of Families

If you have forgotten, here's precisely what Quayle said: "Bearing babies irresponsibly is simply wrong. Failing to support children one has fathered is wrong. We must be unequivocal about this," he said in a speech to the Commonwealth Club of California.

"It doesn't help matters when prime-time TV has Murphy Brown, a character who supposedly epitomizes today's intelligent, highly paid professional woman, mocking the importance of fathers by bearing a child alone and calling it just another lifestyle choice."

I never saw *Murphy Brown*. There's not enough time in the world to make me sit down and waste my life in front of a screen playing that drivel. I don't watch television unless it's to catch *South Park*, a Dallas Cowboys game, or Fox News. But evidently, the main character of this show, played by Candice Bergen, believed having a kid without a father in the picture was just fine. Quayle's speech about "family values" created a huge controversy back in '92. But reading this quote now makes you wonder what the big deal was. His words seem like basic common sense, or maybe they are even prophetic.

Since Quayle had the temerity to point out the need for fathers, the number of single parents in America has skyrocketed. For the first time in the history of the United States, fewer than 60 percent of first-born US babies were brought into this world with a married mother and father. More than one in five first-born children now have parents who are shacking up.[1] Some researchers describe these "fragile families" as only strong enough to create children, but not strong enough to support them. Frequently, these couples break apart after the babies are born.

Do you think this has devastated wealthy forty-something white women like the fictional Murphy Brown? No. Wealthier Americans have a bigger cushion. If they end up with a child out of wedlock, they have high enough salaries and family support that they can usually make it. But poorer people living on a shoestring can't survive high gas prices, much less absorb the expense and complication of another human being. That's the thing about the philosophies that white liberals so casually try to shove down the culture's throat. When they proudly stand up and demand that marriage comes in many different flavors—or, more accurately, that it doesn't matter at all—they're promoting an idea that creates higher risks for poverty, lower educational attainment, and family instability. They are actually hurting poor people, not themselves. Have you ever stopped to ask yourself why college-educated folks are the only demographic left in America that still has children within the benefit of marriage? It's better for the children, for the parents, and for society.

This answer is so obvious that even a liberal buffoon at CNN can see it. After the acquittal of George Zimmerman, Don Lemon went on air with recommendations about how black people can get their acts together. The first one was a doozy:

Black people . . . Just because you can have a baby, it doesn't mean you should. Especially without planning for one or getting married first. More than 72 percent of children in the African-American community are born out of wedlock. That means absent fathers. And the studies show that lack of a male role model is an express train right to prison and the cycle continues.[2]

His comments were even more pointed than those of Dan Quayle, and a black man uttered them. Apparently, Lemon didn't get the memo: liberals don't want black people thinking for themselves. When his speech went viral, other liberals scolded him for "not understanding the plight of black people." But the first thing that happens to a black person when you say anything that doesn't align with Democratic talking points is that your "black card" is revoked. I lost mine a long time ago, and—believe me, Don—it's not worth the price to keep it. An MSNBC host called him a "turncoat." It didn't get better for him. Here are some reprintable versions of tweets[3] he received:

Don Lemon feels that he's THE exception. That's perfectly fine. He'll see eventually how he's viewed by his white counterparts.

@DonLemonCNN must be real THIRSTY for him to try to speak for all AA's and throw our black men under the bus. Are his ratings that bad?

If you follow Don Lemon's 5-step anti-Hip-Hop plan racism magically ends?

I was tired of @donlemoncnn when he was tweeting those wack prosperity sermons every Sunday. Not surprised by this.

Next racial draft we're giving @DonLemonCNN to the whites. I don't even wanna trade him for anyone. Just give him away.

Isn't that a rather strong reaction toward someone who suggested that kids should have moms and dads? Especially when the facts bear out the undeniable truth? A stark difference exists between children raised with both parents and those from a broken home.

One in eight children with two married parents lives below the poverty line, compared to five in ten who are living with a single mom.

Regardless of income, children raised by two parents will have fewer behavioral problems, will be less likely to be hungry or have asthma, and will be more likely to achieve academically.

The principles of faith prevent poverty. Let's face it. God knows a thing or two about the way that humans interact—or the ways they ideally should interact. Though the Bible is not a self-help book, people would be better off if they lived according to the words written on the pages. Proverbs 3:5–6 (ESV) explains how life is made easier by trusting God instead of your emotions: "Trust in the LORD with all your heart, and do not lean on your own understanding. In all your ways acknowledge him, and he will make straight your paths."

Believe me. In all of my years of law enforcement, the people I've encountered would benefit from listening to biblical wisdom, especially as it pertains to marriage.

But you don't have to be a scholar to understand that getting married and staying married lift children and families from poverty. In a *New York Times* article, Annie Lowrey wrote,

> Economists have done studies showing that if you snapped your fingers and suddenly all the country's poor, unmarried partners were hitched . . . the poverty rate would drop. With social trends pushing partners apart, why shouldn't the government push them together—and help end poverty and improve the lot of children while we're at it? It's a rare policy solution that data-crunching geeks and Bible-thumping crusaders can agree on—albeit for very different reasons. Unfortunately, there might not be much that Washington can actually do about it.[4]

Precisely. When the government inserts its nose into a problem, the problem rarely gets better. This is *especially* true about marriage. Can you imagine a worse Cupid than the federal government?

But it's also true about poverty.

War on Poverty

The Heritage Foundation described the complete and abysmal failure of Lyndon B. Johnson's War on Poverty over the past fifty years:

> U.S. taxpayers have spent over $22 trillion on anti-poverty programs. Adjusted for inflation, this spending (which does not include Social Security or Medicare) is three times the cost of all U.S. military wars since the American Revolution. Yet progress against poverty, as measured by the U.S. Census Bureau, has been minimal, and in terms of President Johnson's main goal of reducing the "causes" rather than the mere "consequences"

of poverty, the War on Poverty has failed completely. In fact, a significant portion of the population is now less capable of self-sufficiency than it was when the War on Poverty began.[5]

You can't undo the truth. The Bible is clear: "The one who is unwilling to work shall not eat" (2 Thessalonians 3:10 NIV). But Uncle Sam tries to protect people from the consequences of their own action, or, more honorably, to protect the children of lazy people from their parents' inaction. It makes sense to provide assistance to the infirm. But able-bodied, nonelderly adults should be working or seriously looking for a job before getting a dime of benefits. The Heritage Foundation pointed out what is wrong with giving people something for nothing: "By breaking down the habits and norms that lead to self-reliance, welfare generates a pattern of increasing intergenerational dependence." The writers also pointed out that "by undermining productive social norms, welfare creates a need for even greater assistance in the future."

There are some commonsense ways that the federal government can incentivize marriage and help welfare be distributed to those with an actual need instead of just being lazy. But the government can't fix what is wrong with us as human beings. We need a spiritual solution. As poor, less-educated Americans turn their backs on faith at a far greater rate than wealthy, educated Americans, the culture is splitting wide open. In this nation, those who work hard, finish school, get married, and stay married are very rarely poor. Food stamps, Medicaid, soup kitchens, and good intentions—or even hundreds of billions of government dollars—cannot alone raise people out of poverty.

It's time politicians acknowledged the limitations of government and the role of religion. It's also time we recognize people like Canon Benoît Jayr who faithfully serve God and their communities, one person at a time. They're the real heroes of our nation, even if they wear robes or a clerical collar instead of a cowboy hat, and even if they'd be more likely to pour water over other people's feet than put boots on their own.

Stay Put or Go Home

Most Americans have seen *Roots*, the Alex Haley miniseries aired during the 1970s that detailed the plight of African slave Kunta Kinte. But one scene contains a powerful visual that should speak to us today. Social activist Roland Warren described the scene:

> One day, while Kunta was putting the horses away, he heard a drumbeat that sounded very familiar. So, he followed the beat, and it led him to an old slave. Turns out that this old man was from a tribe in Africa that lived close to Kunta's people. In any case, this man told Kunta to listen for the drumbeat again because it would signal an upcoming escape attempt.
>
> An excited Kunta rushed home to share the news about the drumbeat and the escape with his wife Bell. However, she became very afraid. Her first husband had tried to escape, and he was killed. She said that she did not want to lose Kunta, too. Then, she put his hand on her stomach to feel a baby growing inside of her. Kunta understood and promised not to escape.
>
> When the baby was born, Kunta wanted to dedicate his daughter in the same way his father did for him. One night, he took his swaddled little one outside for the special ceremony. But, as he lifted her into the night sky, he was interrupted by a familiar sound. It was the drumbeats. They were calling to him. He quickly bundled up his little girl and ran toward home. Bell, who was clearly panicked, rushed to meet him. She had heard the drumbeats, too. She approached him quickly and

said, "The drums. ... You ain't gonna run, is you? This is our home." Kunta said defiantly, "This is not my home." Bell's legs buckled as she burst into tears. But then, Kunta steadied his wife, pulled her close as he wrapped his arms around her and said, "But, this is my child, and we are a family!" And, they walked back into their home.[6]

Why am I reminding you of an episode of an old miniseries? Because that scene has a lot of truth in it. As a national figure, I'm frequently asked about how to save this nation. The question, often asked in a public forum, might have a sense of desperation underlying it. As much as I would love to talk about proposals to cut back on entitlements or the Convention of States' plan to restrain the federal government, I know that the answer is much simpler.

I said simpler. Not easy.

As the end of the *Roots* episode described above, Kunta named his daughter Kizzy, which means "stay put" in his native tongue. Warren wrote, "Now, consider what happened here. Kunta Kinte was a married father with no economic rights, no civil rights or rights of any kind. But he had one power that no master's whip could take away. He had the power to stay put, despite the obstacles, risks and challenges, and do everything that he could to provide for and protect his family."

Modern black men have this power too—much more power than this fictional slave had. We live in the greatest nation ever created, with more opportunities than any people group who have ever lived. No matter what you think about our politicians or Black LIES Matter or so-called police brutality, you have the power to improve your life dramatically when you simply "stay put."

Sadly, fathers these days can't even obey this two-word command. They've already left their kids and families. They're out there searching for a better gig, looking for approval in places where it can't be found, trying to find a more interesting path than the boring old domestic life with a wife and kids. But sometimes—almost always—what's boring is the solution. It's called hard work. Personal responsibility.

I was walking down the street one day when a young black man approached me.

"You're Sheriff Clarke, right?" he asked. "I just got out of jail, and I can't get a job."

He then went on to explain the many ways he'd been trying to find employment. It sounded hard. I admit it. Because I have such a close relationship with the criminals in Milwaukee, I'm frequently presented opportunities to speak into their lives. Often, it comes down to a choice between pity and responsibility. I never choose pity. I always choose responsibility. Maybe, more accurately, I always choose the truth. As Martin Luther King Jr. said in his speech "The Other America,"

> I want to discuss the race problem tonight and I want to discuss it very honestly. I still believe that freedom is the bonus you receive for telling the truth. Ye shall know the truth and the truth shall set you free. And I do not see how we will ever solve the turbulent problem of race confronting our nation until there is an honest confrontation with it and a willing search for the truth and a willingness to admit the truth when we discover it.[7]

This guy didn't need anyone to help him wallow in self-pity. And the truth usually has something to do with people taking responsibility for their lives. Right there on the street, I laid some truth on him. Perhaps it was the first time in his life someone made him face reality.

"How many kids do you have?" I asked.

"Three."

"Well, *there's* your job," I said. "Go home and be a great dad so your kids don't end up like you did. You made some lifestyle choices that you are paying for now. Keep working at it, and if you stay determined, something will break for you. But for now, go home and be a good dad to your kids."

He was dumbfounded. "I never looked at it that way," he said. Then after a short conversation, he extended his hand and said, in a softer voice, "Thanks, Sheriff."

Some things can't be done by the government, no matter how well-meaning. All of us are at a critical moment in America's history—blacks, whites, and everyone else. We have the opportunity to choose to be better than the culture demands of us. While the media and politicians will bend over backward to avoid the word *responsibility*, we have to turn from their constant drumbeat of mediocrity and choose another path.

It's a path that many have traveled before. It's a path described most eloquently in the most famous parable in the Bible. The story of the prodigal son tells the story of a young man who asked for his inheritance even before his father died. He left home and partied, slept around, and ended up poor, destitute, lonely, and wondering where his next meal would come from. That's where many are today. But the prodigal son realized he didn't want to be where he was. So he got up and walked home.

Just the word *home* evokes many feelings. I think of being with Julie in our house, where she created a man cave for me in the basement. That's where I can sit and think, dream, and plot my next steps in life. The word also reminds me of that small, well-kept house at 39th and Kaul Avenue, where my mother put food on the table, and we sat down together to eat. It's also the place where my dad stole my shoes at night to make sure I didn't try to sneak out and get into trouble.

Do you see the pattern?

All of us have a tendency to want to sneak away from home and get into trouble. But we also have the opportunity—the moral responsibility—to come back home. Ever hear the phrase "You can't go home again?" Well, that's a lie. Recently, when I was just beginning the process of writing this book, I went back to my old neighborhood to look at the home I'd lived in as a kid. Believe it or not, I couldn't easily locate the house. Maybe it was because I'd never driven to it as a child, or maybe it's because too many years had passed. When my eyes finally settled on that old house, I didn't see the faded, small home that sat next to dozens just like it. In my mind's eye, I saw a place of love, restrictions, discipline, and frustration. A place where I bristled under my dad's constant supervision and the rules I thought were so onerous at the time.

It's true that I couldn't very well pull up to that house and ask the owner to let me in. And even if I did, my toys wouldn't be there; my room wouldn't be the same. My mother's meals wouldn't be on the stove, the wonderful scent beckoning me to come to the table.

Going home doesn't mean literally going back to the place where you were a kid. Sometimes, it means going back to the place you know you should be. When the prodigal son went home, he wasn't sure what to expect. But you know how that story ends:

He arose and came to his father. But when he was still a great way off, his father saw him and had compassion, and ran and fell on his neck and kissed him. And the son said to him, "Father, I have sinned against heaven and in your sight, and am no longer worthy to be called your son."

But the father said to his servants, "Bring out the best robe and put it on him, and put a ring on his hand and sandals on his feet. And bring the fatted calf here and kill it, and let us eat and be merry; for this my son was dead and is alive again; he was lost and is found." And they began to be merry. (Luke 15:20–24 NKJV)

The older brother, who'd stayed on the straight and narrow his whole life, resented the celebration. He complained to his father:

These many years I have been serving you; I never transgressed your commandment at any time; and yet you never gave me a young goat, that I might make merry with my friends. But as soon as this son of yours came, who has devoured your livelihood with harlots, you killed the fatted calf for him. (Luke 15:29 NKJV)

You can just hear the resentment dripping from his voice.

The challenge of the modern American is to begin that journey home. That might mean literally getting in the car and making up with your spouse, going to your kids' baseball games, taking a job you think is beneath you, or even sitting down and eating dinner together. It also might mean going back to the faith that your mother taught you, or apologizing for the thing you did that's been separating you from the ones who love you.

The challenge of modern political and religious leaders is to not be the older brother who resents that the younger brother has problems.

Regardless of whether we are in the "stay put" crowd or the "go home" group, we all need to take assessment of life once we're back at the house. The world doesn't need a bunch of prodigal sons. The world doesn't even really need a bunch of older brothers. Eventually, people have to grow up and mature. Your goal should be to become more like the father in this scenario. All of us—regardless of whether we're parents—need to mature, extend our arms, and welcome the people in this culture who are desperately searching for the ever-elusive place called home.

After all, America is merely a bunch of these homes seemingly connected by miles of dirt roads, blocks of city concrete, or just hallways in an apartment building. What *really* connects these homes into a larger collection that creates a nation has nothing to do with the type of house or the geographic location. What really connects us is our hope that we can do better.

We can—and must—if our nation is to survive. It's time to tune out the constant drumbeat trying to get us to leave the values we've long cherished. It's time to turn off the Internet and our computer screens, to forget the hashtags, and to cherish the people right before us.

It's time to come home, America. The door is open for now. But if we keep maligning, criticizing, and complaining about each other, we might accidentally destroy the very nation many have called home for the past 240 years.

The journey back won't be easy, but it's a path worth taking.

11

God Is Not the Enemy, but He's Being Attacked

"SHERIFF CLARKE?" a man said. I winced but tried to make sure he didn't see it. Julie had gone to a different aisle to get bread. "I just wanted you to know I'm your biggest fan."

I'm very thankful that I've had opportunities and success as the Milwaukee County sheriff. I have to assume that God has put me in this position—one that usually doesn't receive an inordinate amount of attention—for reasons I can't possibly begin to understand. Normally, I'm very grateful for all of the love and support that people give me, but I'm not the guy who loves to be recognized, who needs constant accolades and praise. I'm just a foot soldier, not someone who wants to be in the spotlight. Honestly, it's taken a bit to get used to being recognized in public, and sometimes I just want to get milk and go home.

"Thank you, sir," I said, nodding and moving toward the checkout line. That's when Julie walked up and said, "Hello, how are you?"

I couldn't believe it. Why was she prolonging a conversation with a total stranger? One thing you have to know about my wife is that she is incredibly hardworking. Another is that she loves to chat with people.

"Oh, I've just gotten off work," he said.

I started heading down the aisle when I heard my wife say, "Really? Where do you work?" The woman really doesn't know how to cut off a conversation.

By the time we got into the car, I was flummoxed.

"Why did you stand there and talk and talk?" I asked.

"It was five minutes," she shot back.

The criminals in Milwaukee never even look at me cross-eyed, but I can't tell this little blonde woman anything. She said, "It's called being nice. You should try it sometime."

On the silent drive home, the milk gathering condensation in the backseat, I wondered why she viewed the world so differently. Finally, I just pushed it out of my mind by thinking the one thing I think all the time: she's not a cop; she wouldn't understand.

Hypervigilance Comes Naturally to Cops

Have you ever heard a police officer say something on television or in a movie like this: "I'll ask the questions, ma'am"? That's because cops don't like to be interrogated. The ones asking the questions are the ones with the power. If someone is asking you questions, you are at a disadvantage. Although people who come up to me mean well, it makes me start to bristle. "Did you just get off work?" might be an innocent way to initiate conversation. But a police officer would interpret that as someone trying to get potentially damaging schedule information. We notice things you never would. We're trained to always observe the landscape for things out of place, suspicious activity that might need attention. And one suspicious thing is people asking too many questions.

Every interaction activates cops' sixth sense. It forms our reasonable suspicion that criminal activity may be afoot, that a person may be armed with a weapon and may plan to do us harm. Cops gain experience from constant exposure to this over time. When we do this for, say five to ten years, it becomes second nature. Though it could happen more quickly in urban or high crime areas because of constant exposure, most cops will tell you it takes about five years to become seasoned or truly experienced. This state of constant observation causes us to be hypervigilant, something that could very well save an officer's life. Imagine what I'm like after thirty-eight years of this.

It sometimes drives Julie crazy. Frequently, she'll be telling me a story, and I'll immediately start poking holes in it.

"What do you mean exactly?" I might ask. "I just don't see how that story adds up."

That's when I see the hurt in her eyes and wish I had never said a word.

"I was just trying to tell you what my friend told me about her shopping experience at the mall," she might say. "I didn't realize I had to meet some sort of standard like I'm presenting to a jury."

She's right, of course, but I can't seem to help myself. People lie to police officers so much, we never believe the first thing that comes out of someone's mouth. We expect deception and try to head it off. When Julie starts talking, I don't think, *Okay, David, don't find any faults in this. Just listen and nod.* Instead, my cop nature kicks in and I think, *What's wrong with this story, this statement?* I'm not in other cops' homes, but I've heard other officers say that they sometimes interrogate their kids instead of having a conversation with them. Julie would probably agree that I have that tendency with her.

"Every time I tell you a story," she laments, "you try to find something that's not believable about it."

We don't have to think about being hypervigilant. We just are. Always. The hypervigilance stays activated and doesn't turn off at the end of a tour of duty. That takes its toll on cops' physical, mental, and emotional health. Even off duty, we process everything with a tinge of suspicion. We look for what might not be right about something. Suspicion is good when we're looking at evidence and suspects, but it can be problematic with family and friends. If we're not conscious of it, we'll become cynical about everything.

I always stand with my right hip away from people when I talk because that's where I keep my weapon holstered. For almost four decades, I've been aware of weapon retention, so it's become second nature to turn slightly away from people when talking. Do people perceive this interview stance to be stand-offish? Perhaps, but it's just a natural by-product of training. All humans need personal space, but cops tend to keep people at arm's length. We let in only certain people. Spouses and kids, of course, don't have to ask to invade personal space. But we don't want anyone else in there. We're trained to survive in the field. When a random guy at the grocery store puts his hand on my arm, I realize I can't easily turn it off.

It should surprise no one that cops are profane. If a cop can trust you with his life, he's going to assume he can trust that you won't be overly sensitive about language. Instead of saying, "Move over, please," a cop might phrase the request to his partner in a much harsher, even vulgar, way. It's just the way some police officers communicate. The challenge is that a cop might slip and say something like this in off-duty life and seem incredibly rude.

It's natural for officers to begin to withdraw from people who don't understand why we are the way we are, and for many cops to exclusively hang out with our own kind. For better or worse—or like most things, both—a circle-the-wagons mentality sets in. Hanging out with other officers cuts through a lot of the hassle of relationships. Cops understand each other so we don't have to spend a lot of time explaining our unique proclivities.

I have rarely hung out with other cops off duty. I've never been on cop bowling leagues, or dart leagues, or participated in card game socials. That wasn't by design; I just had different interests. That separation helped but did not totally cure me from that state of hypervigilance. I'm more hypervigilant today after all my years of service than I've ever been. The politics of my job taught me that politics is a cutthroat business.

In early May 2006, George Papachristou, a former Milwaukee police officer who was involved in a deadly-use-of-force incident, contacted me with an idea. He told me about a new faith-based support group he was organizing for police officers.

Papachristou's organization was faith-based, nondenominational, and strictly voluntary. You could be a Christian, belong to another faith, or have no faith at all. Elmbrook Church in Brookfield, Wisconsin, sponsored the group designed to help police officers deal with their unique set of concerns, habits, and problems. The suicide rate for police officers is three times the rate for civilians, as are the rates of alcoholism and divorce. Police officers have life expectancies ten years less than the average person. It was intriguing to me that a new group existed to provide emotional and physical support for police to receive the understanding and help they need.

Roll Call and Community Groups

We hold roll call every morning at the office when all of the officers on shift duty get together to make sure everyone is on the same page about crime trends and are properly equipped. I'd gotten in the habit of inviting groups from the community into our office during roll call to inspire my officers. Some of these groups have a faith element while others do not. Over the course of my time as sheriff, we had a number of organizations meet with us.

In other words, I didn't care about the religious background or political viewpoint of the group. I just cared whether it could inspire police officers. I wanted them to hear the best of a wide variety of views. After all, if we protect freedom, I believe in practicing freedom. One of the groups I invited was the Centurions.

The Centurions—a reference to cops as guardians—dealt specifically with the concerns and struggles of police officers and served as a peer support group. And so, they presented to the officers throughout the month, offering encouragement and advice. Two police officers—Ilir Sino (a Muslim) and Mark Zidek (a Catholic)—didn't like these presentations. They and their union, the Milwaukee Deputy Sheriffs' Association, brought an action against Captain Edward Bailey and me in our official capacities, as well as Milwaukee County.[1] They claimed listening to the Centurions' talk during roll call was a violation of the establishment clause and the free exercise clause of the First Amendment. Not only did they seek an injunction to prevent future presentations from the Centurions at department events; they sought damages. Imagine my reaction. *No good deed goes unpunished.*

I didn't understand why it was a big deal. If I had refused to let the Centurions speak based solely on their religious point of view, I'd be violating their rights, correct? Besides, no one says things that everyone likes. We don't have a right not to be offended, and if the officers disliked the message one day, they may love a different speaker the next day. I argued that the First Amendment's free speech clause provided a defense to the establishment clause claim. How could I possibly be violating the cops' rights when I wasn't discriminating in my speaker choices? Is religious speech actually disfavored in this country? Do the religious have fewer rights than the nonreligious?

When both sides filed motions for summary judgment, the district court sided with the plaintiffs, and the Seventh Circuit Court of Appeals affirmed. Turns out, Judge Ann Claire Williams—who happened to be appointed by Ronald Reagan—was not happy with me. In her opinion, she wrote that "the Centurions also provided a benefit to the officers in the form of a support group. But their unique faith-based approach sets them apart from the secular organizations invited to speak. The Centurions offered peer support, but also sought to foster discussion on how the officers could 'impact others for Christ' and on Christ's impact in their lives." She went on to write:

> In this case, the Centurions gave a heavily Christian-focused presentation at a mandatory conference for government employees, and the Sheriff subsequently invited them to present at mandatory roll calls during work hours, granting them unfiltered access to a captive audience of subordinates. At each roll call, they were personally introduced by the Sheriff's command staff and were permitted to distribute additional Christian-focused literature. Even more telling was the Sheriff's refusal to cease the presentations after some of the deputies complained of the Centurions' proselytizing. He took no steps to disentangle himself or the Department from any of the religious messages, . . . and his actions, at the least, appeared to place the Centurions in the same category as the other "partnering" organizations, like Johnson's Bike Company—all of whom presumably received the Department's approval.[2]

The court awarded the plaintiffs $38,687.41 in attorneys' fees. Thankfully, they only awarded $1 in damages to each plaintiff. The case had taken so much of a toll on me that I had to talk to my spiritual advisor who, at the time, was the archbishop of Milwaukee and is now the cardinal of the New York diocese.

Though I lost this case, I learned important lessons, and I'm still fighting. Unfortunately, we live in an era when some people will make even God the enemy. This is particularly sad, since God is the only answer to our deep-seated concerns and issues. With my own eyes I've seen God make a difference in cops' lives. It makes no sense to discriminate against the Christian message. It's an injustice. Supreme Court Justice Clarence Thomas said it might be time to revisit this case.

One thing is certain. The legal battle that I went through gave me much compassion and appreciation for Christians who are fighting for their rights in legal battles that will help determine the flavor and shape of our nation in years to come. People are losing their businesses and facing heavy fines because they live out their faith. And if you think that these stories are the exception, and that you are immune to this type of discrimination, you are wrong. Three examples tell the concerning condition of religious freedom in this nation.

The ACLU Loves You, The ACLU Loves You Not . . .

Barronelle Stutzman has been a florist in Richland, Washington, for three decades. During that time, she's met many people—both customers and employees—but one client in particular stood out. Customer Rob Ingersoll loved flowers the way that Barronelle did, with the eye of an artist.

"We see not just potential bouquets, but how different combinations and just-right arrangements can bring a special beauty, memories and even a little humor to someone's birthday, anniversary—or wedding," she said. "For 10 years, we encouraged that artistry in each other."[3]

Barronelle knew Rob was gay; he knew she was a Christian. Their differences weren't a hindrance to their friendship. Baronelle had employed people who identified as gay. But one day Rob came in and told her that he was getting married to his same-sex partner and wanted her to design something special for their wedding.

"If all he'd asked for were prearranged flowers, I'd gladly have provided them. If the celebration were for his partner's birthday, I'd have been delighted to pour my best into the challenge. But as a Christian, weddings have a particular significance," she explained. "Marriage does celebrate two people's love for one another, but its sacred meaning goes far beyond that. Surely without intending to do so, Rob was asking me to choose between my affection for him and my commitment to Christ. As deeply fond as I am of Rob, my relationship with Jesus is everything to me."

She wasn't ashamed of her faith, but she described that conversation as one of the most difficult of her life. She gave him the names of three other florists who would create something beautiful for him and his partner, Curt Freed. Rob told Barronelle that he understood, and she believed they parted as friends.

She was surprised when the two men, represented by the American Civil Liberties Union (ACLU), sued her. (The Washington state attorney general has also sued Baronelle, and as I am writing this, the Washington Supreme Court is days from oral arguments commencing on the case.) "We are saddened that we were denied service by Arlene's Flowers after doing business with them and valuing their services for so many years. We respect others' religious values, but being discriminated against was hurtful and illegal," they wrote in a joint statement.

"This business has broken the law, and should be held accountable. We appreciate the support from people across the globe, and look forward to having this issue resolved."[4]

This case, however, isn't really about refusing service on the basis of sexual orientation. She'd sold flowers to Rob for years and even helped him find another florist. Rob and his partner got so many offers of flowers that they could've done twenty weddings at no cost.

In spite of this, they're trying to intimidate and harass Barronelle to use her God-given talents in ways that compromise her Christian beliefs. Interestingly, they sued her in her business capacity and in her personal capacity, which puts her at great risk. The statutes allow the ACLU and the state to collect attorney fees, which will be six to seven figures. In other words, all of her assets are at issue. Because the ACLU and state can create the precedent they want by just suing her business, going after her personally was spiteful and unnecessary. Not only could she lose her business, she could lose everything because she refused to provide flowers for a same-sex wedding that had plenty of flowers from other vendors.

"I want to believe that a state as diverse as Washington, with our long commitment to personal and religious freedoms, would be as willing to honor my right to make those kinds of choices as it is to honor Rob's right to make his," Barronelle said. "That's not endorsing a negative thing as I've been accused of doing. It's promoting good things: reason, fairness and mutual tolerance. I don't think that's too much to ask of a court of law—or from a friend I dearly miss."

This case has taken a toll on Barronelle's life. She's had to stop doing all weddings during the lawsuit because of the liability exposure. She's lost what she enjoys most about floral design as well as all of the referrals a florist gets from weddings. Those referrals are extremely helpful to a business and allow florists to serve customers from cradle to grave.

Beyond that, she's had death threats, threats to burn down her business, and threats against her computer network. For a while, she had to drive different routes to work, hire computer specialists to create a protective firewall, and install security cameras. When the news of the case broke, her local community was extremely supportive. However, activists from around the nation e-mailed and called her. Paying customers had a hard time getting through to place an order since activists swearing, threatening, and generally harassing her deluged her business with calls.

It's hard to believe all of this is directed at a seventy-year-old florist because of her deeply held religious beliefs. It's even harder to imagine that this is happening in America.

Baby-Killing Drugs or
Business-Killing Boycotts

In 1944, Ralph Stormans opened his first store at the Grand Central Public Market, the first large supermarket in Olympia, Washington. It quickly grew but was replaced in 1956 by an expanded version called Ralph's Thriftway. In 1977, the family purchased Bailey Drugs, and the thriving store still offers groceries and medicine to its community.

But not *all* medicine. The Stormanses declined to sell abortifacients, or drugs that cause a miscarriage by killing a fertilized egg. When customers request a drug like Plan B, the Stormanses refer them to one of the more than thirty other pharmacies within a five-mile radius. (Convenient for the customers, but very inconvenient for the unborn baby.) The Stormanses' decision not to sell those drugs didn't prohibit one person from acquiring the drug of choice.

"But to anti-Christian bigots, it is intolerable that Christian professionals exist unless they bow the knee to the Baal of the sexual revolution," First Amendment attorney David French wrote. "So Washington's governor took action—demanding that the Washington State Board of Pharmacy issue regulations that required pharmacists to issue abortifacients regardless of religious or moral objections."[5]

Notably, the state has never investigated any pharmacy for a failure to stock a drug in the forty-five-year history of the stock rule. Also, ten times as many pharmacies don't stock this drug because it's not profitable enough than those that won't stock it for moral reasons. Though the state does nothing to the pharmacies that don't stock it for financial reasons, they investigated the Stormanses for ten years straight.

All over the nation, Christian pharmacists had a choice—to comply with these new regulations or close their doors. This, of course, could have negative repercussions throughout the nation. Some small mom-and-pop pharmacies serve areas that aren't as packed with pharmacy options as Olympia, Washington. When they close their doors, patients have fewer options and less access to the drugs they need.

The Ninth Circuit sided with the state, and the sorry Supreme Court declined to hear what French described as the most "plainly vicious anti-Christian cases I've ever seen."[6] Thirty-five pharmacy organizations—both local and national—support the Stormanses' right of conscience. None support the state.

Like Barronelle, the Stormanses have paid dearly for their stand. The governor, state legislators, and pro-abortion groups have boycotted their business; they've had to hire security guards after activists blocked their streets and entrances. Activist groups sent in fake test shoppers who pretended to want to purchase the morning-after pill. With every test shopper's complaint, the state launched a new investigation, the media picked it up, and the protests began anew.

The state has said the Stormanses are in "outright defiance" of state law, and board members have testified that they will revoke the pharmacy's license if a complaint for a failure to stock Plan B is filed.

The Stormanses rely heavily on the pharmacy for their business because a significant number of shoppers come to the store for their medicine. Not only do they fill prescriptions, but the shoppers frequently buy groceries while waiting for their prescriptions to be filled. Because of this morning-after pill controversy, their business revenue has plummeted 30 percent.

Your Off-Duty Faith May Cost Your Job!

Chief Kelvin Cochran had the kind of employment history that would inspire books or a Hallmark movie. Born into deep poverty in the segregated South, Cochran was one of six children. When his alcoholic father left home never to return, his mother was faced with the daunting task of raising her children alone. She took them to church and taught them to love America. They ate mayonnaise sandwiches and—if they wanted dessert—made "sugar water" for a sweet treat (just sugar in tap water). One day, a neighbor's house caught fire, and Kelvin watched in awe as a big red fire truck arrived to save the day. At church, he was taught that he could do anything he wanted to do in America. Even though the Shreveport Fire Department was completely white, he believed them.

In 1981, Kelvin achieved his childhood goal of becoming a firefighter. He was only the eighth or ninth black person to be hired at the Shreveport Fire Department. Soon, he was promoted to Shreveport's fire training officer, then to assistant chief training officer. He was soon a captain in the training academy, appointed assistant chief, and then became the first black fire chief of the Shreveport Fire Department.

In 2008, Cochran was recruited to become Atlanta's fire chief.

This career trajectory would be enough to make anyone proud. But the following year, President Obama appointed him as the US fire administrator for the United States Fire Administration, a division of the Federal Emergency Management Agency. After his stint there, he learned that Atlanta's department had been unsettled by budget cuts and low morale. In 2010, he happily returned to Atlanta to revitalize the department and faithfully serve as fire chief. His hard work paid off. *Fire Chief* magazine named him "Fire Chief of the Year." In 2014, Atlanta earned a Public Protection Classification rating of Class 1 from the Insurance Services Office. For the first time in the city's history, it received this rating because of the "exemplary ability to respond to fires."[7]

Cochran, who is a Christian, sometimes led Bible studies in his off-duty hours, including a study group called Quest for Authentic Manhood. During that study, he noticed what God asked Adam in the Garden of Eden after he and Eve sinned: "Who told you that you were naked?" Cochran believed "naked" could be a metaphor for how many of us live today—"condemned and deprived." But God didn't leave us in that state. Instead, he clothed, redeemed, and restored us. Only God can offer us the dignity and redemption that people crave and need.

He decided to write a book on this topic, but first he asked the city of Atlanta's ethics officer for advice. Were there any ethical or regulatory problems with a city employee penning a "non-work-related, faith-based book"? He said she responded that it was fine as long as it didn't deal with the "city government or fire department."[8]

He wrote in the mornings before work and in his limited spare time over the weekends. He self-published the 162-page book in late 2013. Only six of those pages dealt with sex and sexuality, in which he advocated for the traditional Christian perspective on the topic: sex should be enjoyed within the benefit of a male-female marriage. It seems silly to point this out, but perhaps I should considering the strangeness of the times: Cochran's position echoes every orthodox Protestant denomination in the United States and every Catholic church.

Over the next year, Cochran handed out his book to people with whom he'd already discussed their Christian faith, to the mayor, to a few members of the Atlanta city council. No one complained about the book until one employee showed the sexuality pages to a gay city council member. The city council member took the book to Atlanta's human resources commissioner, and things got complicated fast.

The mayor publicly excoriated Cochran by saying, "I profoundly disagree with and am deeply disturbed by the sentiments expressed in the paperback regarding the LGBT community. I want to be clear that the material in Chief Cochran's book is not representative of my personal beliefs and is inconsistent with the administration's work to make Atlanta a more welcoming city for all of her citizens—regardless of their sexual orientation, gender, race, and religious beliefs." He went on to say that he'd make Cochran complete "sensitivity training."

Not one single fire department employee complained of mistreatment or discrimination, yet Cochran was fired. Let's take a moment to appreciate the irony here. Cochran was fired because of his off-duty religious viewpoint to prove that Atlanta was . . . welcoming of all viewpoints. *National Review* summed this up nicely: "The lesson here is clear. If you believe you are safe from the new thought police, you are wrong. Cochran fought discrimination his entire life. Cochran was an Obama appointee in the Department of Homeland Security. Cochran made a concerted effort to include his LGBT employees. Cochran was fired."[9]

But here's the thing. Sometimes even when you lose, you win. How? By bringing greater attention to the crisis of religious freedom in this country. I've been a cop long enough to know that things don't always go your way. There are bad days on the job, and there are bad days in any political fight. But I also know that only cowards desert the field of battle. Here's what brave people do: they support the people who fight and lose, they don't get cocky or arrogant when they win, and they just keep fighting. The people who've declared war on God don't stop. Why should people of faith?

12

Homeland Security Equals Personal Security

SAMY MOHAMED HAMZEH worked at Round Kickboxing Gym in downtown Milwaukee, where he led classes. According to his students, he was a pretty nice guy, if not very chatty. "He was always encouraging and always pushing us to go harder," one client said. Little did the kickboxing students know their trainer had more in store for Milwaukee residents than toning their legs.

After losing his kickboxing job—his boss said he was too intense—Hamzeh and two friends went to a historic building on North Van Buren Street in Milwaukee. Originally built in 1889 as a Romanesque Revival church, it has been a Masonic Temple since 1912 and a popular gathering place for conferences, weddings, parties, and meetings. According to the FBI, Hamzeh and his friends hoped to pull off a terror-type attack that would make headlines across the globe, so they took a tour to scout their target. They planned to cover their heads and enter the building where they'd first come in contact with the receptionist. "If she was alone, it is okay, if there were two of them, shoot both of them," Hamzeh instructed his friends, and "do not let the blood show, shot [sic] her from the bottom, two or three shots in her stomach and let her sit on the chair and push her to the front, as if she is sleeping."[1]

After shooting the secretary, they planned on locking the event-goers inside the building. "One of us will stay at the door at the entrance and lock the door down, he will be at the main door down, two will get to the lift (elevator) up, they will enter the room, and spray everyone in the room," he said. "The one who is standing downstairs will spray anyone he finds."

They wanted "to annihilate everyone . . . when we go into a room, we will be killing everyone, that's it, this is our duty." But he conceded he might not be able to kill everyone. "Thirty is excellent. If I got out, after killing thirty people, I will be happy 100 percent . . . because these 30 will terrify the world." He warned them not to overreact after the shootings occurred. "We leave, as if there is nothing, no running, no panic, just regular walking."

Thankfully, Hamzeh was just as idiotic as he was evil. Before launching the attack, he needed three automatic weapons with silencers. Posing as gun sellers, undercover FBI agents showed Hamzeh two automatic weapons and a silencer that he accepted. Once the weapons were in his car, they arrested him.

Think about that. The FBI sold this man guns and let him drive off. What if he started a high-speed chase? What if he turned his brand spanking new guns on the agents?

Good thing he didn't ask for a bomb!

So why did the FBI agents go as far as selling these potential terrorists guns? It's not because they like to risk their lives. Rather, they have to meet the burden of proof required by the court system. Even in the post-9/11 world, the FBI operates under a law-enforcement model that seeks probable cause to arrest, a very high standard often not achievable until *after* an attack occurs. The agency needs enough evidence that the charge will stand up in a court of law. However, the mission of a true intelligence agency is to disrupt, prevent, and detect terror attacks before they occur. An arrest is not necessarily the goal. Informing decision makers in enough time to act is the goal.

Only when the FBI agents moved in did this criminal, this wannabe terrorist, realize his two friends were informants secretly recording their Arabic conversations for the government. He was not charged with terror-related charges under the police model. Instead he was charged only with possessing a machine gun and a silencer. So after all that work, this goof was charged with a lesser crime, even though he was trying to terrorize Milwaukee and America.

Here's where we get it wrong. These people, whether part of an international organization or radicalized American citizens, are *not* common criminals. They're enemy combatants.

As soon as the FBI realized this guy was planning an attack, a prevention mind-set demands that the would-be-terrorist should be picked up and held indefinitely. Under a wartime model, we would have had enough to snatch this guy, charge him with treason, and hold him as an enemy combatant. But what we ended up with here is a less-than-satisfying result. It's time for our agencies to realize that we *are at war* with ISIS and need to change from a law-enforcement model to a wartime model.

As a law-enforcement leader who is on the front lines dealing with domestic terrorism and attacks on our population, I want to relay one crucial bit of intelligence: we are not structured properly and thus are unable to defend the homeland adequately until our domestic intelligence apparatus changes drastically.

Yes, this Milwaukee attack was thwarted, but the absence of an attack does not mean other threats have disappeared. FBI Director James Comey stated in 2015 that his "caseload of ISIS suspects has exploded to more than 900 in all 50 states."[2] Let that sink in. Former New York City Mayor Rudy Giuliani, speaking at the Values Voters Summit in Washington, DC, two days before the fifteenth anniversary of 9/11, said, "If you asked me this on the fifth or sixth anniversary of 9/11, I'd say our job of security had somewhat improved . . . but since President Obama and Hillary Clinton [have been in power]—and I don't mean to be political—our national security has deteriorated. Our country is in more danger today than on 9/11."[3]

For the first time since the world wars, local authorities like me have to think about global issues that are invading our communities. We play an important role in protecting the American people from threats that can affect the economic, physical, and psychological well-being of the country.

Before the September 11, 2001, attacks, the United States didn't even have an executive department with a first priority of defending America from domestic attack. When the 9/11 Commission studied the worst terrorist attack in world history, it assessed the conditions, the agencies, the environment, and the series of events that may have led to the tragedy. One finding from the commission was that a reorganization of the intelligence community was needed.

That was the wrong conclusion.

Congress created an entire new federal agency, the Department of Homeland Security (DHS), to deal with protecting the borders, securing transportation, immigration, Customs Service, critical infrastructure, and organizing assistance to critical incidents. The idea was to unify homeland security efforts and reject the former patchwork approach. Fusions Centers and Joint Terrorism Task Forces were created at the state and local levels to improve collection, analysis, reporting and sharing of information among local law enforcement agencies, the FBI, and the DHS. This relationship coordinated by DHS would make state and local law enforcement a new player in counterterrorism investigations. Efficiency was the goal. Confusion was the result.

If you are puzzled about the differences of responsibility among the CIA, the FBI, DHS, and local police, you aren't alone. Nobody else can make sense of this dysfunctional bureaucracy. The 9/11 Commission report recommended the FBI take on the added responsibility of domestic terrorism. While the FBI has had its successes, it's not ideal to put a law enforcement entity as the lead agency responsible for acts of war within our borders. The FBI's culture and design are to gather evidence for arrest and prosecution, not ongoing intelligence production. The FBI has a cultural tendency to err on the side of doing *everything* by the book, which is advantageous in many respects. For example, their respect for compliance with the law safeguards our privacy and civil liberties. But that tendency, coupled with the lack of a formal mechanism to share information among agencies, has caused critical problems. *Stovepiping* is the term used to describe the phenomenon by which information travels up and down within an organization but shares little horizontally among organizations. It's hard to break down stovepipes when there are so many stoves that are legally and politically entitled to have cast iron pipes of their own. Sad to say, this frustrates the objective of the 9/11 Commission to replace a "need to know" culture with a "need to share" culture.

The sheer number of attacks on American soil exposes a central problem with our domestic counterterrorism efforts: the wrong agency is handling our domestic intelligence. A true intelligence mind-set warns decision makers about the ones threatening us, their capabilities, and whether they are planning an attack. The arrest of the suspect is secondary. This has nothing to do with the fine work of FBI agents, but this organization is designed around building cases to prosecute rather than producing pure intelligence to detect and prevent large-scale terror planning.

In organizing its counterterrorism efforts domestically through the FBI, the US government continues to use a law-enforcement model organized around not taking action until evidence exists to make an arrest for prosecution. That is inefficient and ineffective. It has proven dangerous in its inability to stop terrorism on our home soil. We are at war. Homegrown radicalization has the enemy inside our borders. Islamist-radicalized Americans are not criminals. They are enemy combatants. Our criminal justice system should not prosecute them. Military tribunals should process them.

Since the September 11 attacks, we've had more than our share of these attacks.

Timeline of Attacks

YEAR: 2002

LOCATION*:* Los Angeles Airport

KILLED: 2

WOUNDED: 4

TERRORIST: Hesham Mohamed Hadayet, an Egyptian national

WHAT HAPPENED: The Fourth of July was Hesham Mohamed Hadayet's birthday. On that day, he walked into the Los Angeles International Airport and found the El Al ticket counter. There, Hadayet killed two Israelis and wounded four others before the Israeli airline's security guard managed to shoot and kill him. He didn't seem to be formally connected to a specific terrorist group, but he had expressed opposition to America's policy in the Middle East, declared anti-Jewish sentiment, and hoped his actions would influence our government to become more pro-Palestinian.[4]

YEAR: 2006

LOCATION: Seattle, Washington

KILLED: 1

WOUNDED: 5

TERRORIST: Naveed Haq, a Pakistani-American

WHAT HAPPENED: Haq walked into the Jewish Federation of Greater Seattle, a group that raises money for social welfare initiatives, supports Israel, and runs educational programs for the local community. Witnesses say he was complaining about American policies toward Israel and Jews as he opened fire on the victims. He surrendered only after talking with a 911 operator who explained to him that she could not connect him with CNN.[5]

YEAR: 2009

LOCATION: Little Rock, Arkansas

KILLED: 1

WOUNDED: 1

TERRORIST: Abdulhakim Mujahid Muhammad (born Carlos Bledsoe), a US citizen

WHAT HAPPENED: Bledsoe lived in Memphis when he converted to Islam at a Tennessee mosque. After changing his name and traveling in the Middle East, he became radicalized. On June 1, 2009, Muhammad drove his black Ford Explorer Sport Trac by a military recruitment office and opened fire with a rifle, hoping to kill as many military personnel as possible.

(He managed to kill one soldier and wound another.) He said he was "mad at the U.S. military because of what they had done to Muslims in the past."[6]

YEAR: 2009

LOCATION: Fort Hood, Texas

KILLED: 13

WOUNDED: 32

TERRORIST: Maj. Nidal Hasan, a US Army psychiatrist

WHAT HAPPENED: On November 5, 2009, Hasan shouted, "Allahu Akbar!" in a medical facility at the Fort Hood military base as he opened fire with a high-powered, high-capacity handgun. Military police shot him and paralyzed him from the waist down, but not before he fired more than two hundred rounds.[7]

YEAR: 2013

LOCATION: Boston Marathon

KILLED: 3

WOUNDED: 264[8]

TERRORISTS: Dzhokhar Tsarnaev and Tamerlan Tsarnaev, Chechen brothers

WHAT HAPPENED: On April 15, 2013, two pressure cooker bombs detonated twelve seconds apart near the Boylston Street finish line of the Boston Marathon. Three days later, investigators identified the two suspects and released their photos to the public. The two shot and killed police officer Sean Collier on the campus of the Massachusetts Institute of Technology, hijacked a car, and led the police on a chase. Eventually, police shot and killed Tamerlan and later arrested Dzhokhar.

YEAR: 2014

LOCATION: Vaughan Foods in Oklahoma

KILLED: 1

WOUNDED: 1

TERRORIST: Alton Nolen

WHAT HAPPENED: On September 25, 2014, an employee at Vaughan Foods named Alton Nolen was suspended from his job. He went back into the plant and beheaded a fifty-four-year-old woman with a knife and injured another woman. (According to police, Nolen admitted this.) His Facebook page's jihadist images and his desire to convert coworkers to Islam spurred an FBI investigation. (Nolen had recently converted to Islam.)[9] Greg Mashburn, the district attorney for Cleveland County, said Nolen used "some Arabic terms during the attack."

Mashburn addressed the issue of what the state could do in this case: "There is not a terrorism statute in the state of Oklahoma." Then he pointed out that the federal authorities would have to be the ones to deal with it."

YEAR: 2014

LOCATION: Washington and New Jersey

KILLED: 4

WOUNDED: 0

TERRORIST: Ali Muhammad Brown

WHAT HAPPENED: The Seattle man confessed to the murder of three men in Washington state and the murder of a college student in New Jersey to seek revenge for America's Middle East policy.

"My mission is my mission between me and my lord.

That's it," Brown said. "My mission is vengeance, for the lives, millions of lives are lost every day."

YEAR: 2015

LOCATION: Chattanooga, Tennessee

KILLED: 5

WOUNDED: 2

TERRORIST: Mohammad Abdulazeez

WHAT HAPPENED: On July 16, 2015, Abdulazeez did a drive-by shooting at a recruiting center in Chattanooga, Tennessee. Then he drove to a US Navy Reserve center and continued the mayhem. Four marines died right there, while a sailor, a marine recruiter, and a police officer were wounded and taken to the hospital. The sailor died two days later.

Following an FBI investigation, Director James B. Comey said Abdulazeez committed these atrocious killings because he was "motivated by foreign terrorist organization propaganda."

YEAR: 2015

LOCATION: Inland Regional Center in San Bernardino, California

KILLED: 14

WOUNDED: 21

TERRORISTS: Syed Rizwan Farook (American citizen of Pakistani descent), his wife Tashfeen Malik (who entered on a K-1 visa), and Enrique Marquez Jr. (Farook's former neighbor, who converted to Islam).

WHAT HAPPENED: On December 2, 2015, American-born Syed Rizwan Farook and his wife, Tashfeen Malik, went on a shooting spree at the county health department Christmas party being held in a rented banquet room for about eighty employees. Farook worked at the department, and his wife accompanied him to the event. She had posted a pledge of allegiance to ISIS on Facebook the day of the attack. After the attack, they left in a rented SUV. Four hours later, police killed them in a shootout. FBI Director James B. Comey said that their investigation revealed that the perpetrators were "home-grown violent extremists" inspired by foreign terrorist groups.

YEAR: 2016

LOCATION: Pulse Nightclub in Orlando, Florida

KILLED: 49

WOUNDED: 53

TERRORIST: Omar Mateen, a New York-born American citizen

WHAT HAPPENED: It was almost last call at the gay night-club called Pulse when a gunman opened fire on the crowd. The shooting lasted as long as the duration of a song. But by the time it was over, forty-nine people were dead, and fifty-three were wounded in the worst mass shooting in American history. FBI agent Ronald Hopper said, "We do have suggestions that that individual may have leanings towards that, that particular ideology." The "particular ideology" was jihadism. Mateen called 911 while holding the hostages and pledged allegiance to ISIS, so that should be a pretty good clue as to his motivation.

YEAR: 2016

LOCATION: Chelsea neighborhood in New York and Seaside Park, New Jersey

KILLED: 0

WOUNDED: 29

TERRORIST: Ahmad Khan Rahami, a naturalized citizen born in Afghanistan

WHAT HAPPENED: Two bombs, planted in the Chelsea neighborhood of Manhattan, were made with pressure cookers, flip phones, and Christmas lights. One went off, injuring twenty-nine, but the other didn't detonate. Meanwhile, in Seaside, New Jersey, a bomb went off in a garbage can near a Marine Corps charity run. It was set to go off during the race, but logistical problems delayed the start of the race. No one was injured, but had the bomb gone off just a few minutes later, marines would've been running by the garbage can. Investigators found three rudimentary pipe bomb–type devices, but only one detonated. Rahami faces charges in both New York and New Jersey in connection with these incidents.

Steps for Protecting Ourselves

All the incidents mentioned above are intelligence failures that should be evaluated further to make sure they don't happen again. Though I don't want to offer a comprehensive domestic terror plan in this book, we can make seven behavior changes that will go a long way in protecting us.

1. Stop ignoring the vivid flashing signs of trouble. The FBI admitted that Omar Mateen was on the radar as a person of interest well before the Pulse nightclub shootings. In 2013, the agency questioned him after his coworkers reported Mateen made comments that seemed too sympathetic to terrorists. In 2014, agents learned he'd been communicating with an American who later died in a Syrian suicide bombing. In both cases, the agency shut down the investigations because no laws were broken.

The Boston attack by the Tsarnaev brothers occurred because national security agencies failed to connect the dots. There were several signs: Russian intelligence agencies notified their American counterparts that one of the brothers had visited Chechnya, a hotbed of terror training camps; the brothers were visiting jihadist websites and spewing jihadist rhetoric; and they used a credit card to purchase bomb-making materials. These red flags occurred long before the bombing. To top it off, federal agencies responsible for preventing terror attacks didn't share any of this information with local police, believing this information didn't rise to the level of suspicion. They should have shared it with the Boston Police Department and let them determine its credibility and likelihood. However, the Tsarnaev brothers were able to openly plan and execute their terror attack in Boston with no fear of being watched. This included traveling to a hotbed of terror training camps in Chechnya, a country from which they fled for their lives and sought and were granted asylum here in America.

We also should've seen the looming threat of Nidal Hasan before he killed thirteen at Fort Hood. Did you know he once was asked to give a lecture about a medical issue but proceeded to present to the other doctors an extremist interpretation of the Koran? In his speech, he said all non-Muslims were "non-believers" and so should be set on fire and sent to hell. He also said they should be decapitated and have boiling oil poured down their throats. His fellow doctors reported that Hasan attempted to convert them, and he said he was a "Muslim first and American second."[10] Others reported that he viewed his postgraduate classes at the Uniformed Service University in Bethesda, Maryland, as opportunities to convert people to Islam.

Others were said to be too afraid to offend Hasan by speaking out, but at least one of his fellow doctors reported Hasan for his "anti-American rants." Dr. Val Finnell said, "The system is not doing what it's supposed to do. He at least should have been confronted about these beliefs, ordered to cease and desist, and told to shape up or ship out. I really questioned his loyalty."

There were literally signs that no one heeded, including a note on his business card that described him as "SOA" or "slave," or another interpretation was "soldier of Allah."

Military activist Hasan had been communicating with bomb maker Anwar al-Awlaki, a radical cleric known for his incendiary anti-American ideology and his support of al-Qaeda. Intelligence agencies had intercepted their messages but determined there was nothing to worry about. No one batted an eye when Hasan described the war against the Taliban in Afghanistan and al-Qaeda in Iraq as "a war on Islam."[11] Or even when he often said he should quit the military since the Koran forbids alliances with Jews or Christians. He believed if he were killed while fighting against Muslims, he would go to hell.

As political activist Selena Coppa, said, "This man was a psychiatrist and was working with other psychiatrists every day and they failed to notice how deeply disturbed someone right in their midst was." I believe a more accurate statement would be that people saw the warning signs but were too afraid to commit a sin against political correctness.

Perhaps the biggest flashing indication that the system is broken is the Phoenix memo. On July 10, 2001, a Phoenix FBI agent wrote a memo about Middle Eastern men who were attending flight school. The memo warned of a possible "effort by Usama bin Laden to send students to the U.S. to attend civil aviation universities and colleges." The agent was concerned because men in an Arizona flight school were learning only how to *land* the plane, not to *take off*. That seemed suspicious, but even though the memo was circulated to about a dozen FBI agents, it was promptly ignored. FBI Director Robert Mueller saw it *after* September 11 after these men had become some of the hijackers on that fateful day that changed our nation forever.

We cannot refuse to see the signs right in front of our eyes, and we need a way to easily share information among law-enforcement groups to prevent further disasters.

2. No longer accept the FBI's lame excuse. When that rudimentary bomb went off in Chelsea, local politicians rushed to calm fears by parsing over whether it was an act of international terror or a lone-wolf attack. As if that matters. In short order the FBI announced that an arrest had been made, which signaled to someone like me in law en-forcement that we would learn the suspect Ahmad Khan Rahami was previously known to the FBI.

Sure enough. He was.

We're told that no probable cause existed to arrest Rahami before he attacked. We have seen this response again and again. There comes a point when we have to ask for accountability from those tasked with this job. Right now, the FBI is the lead domestic security agency. We learned, as in nearly every other attack, the agency looked but found no probable cause to arrest and turned away.

Continuing to ask the FBI to handle domestic security is wrong-headed and dangerous because the FBI is culturally structured to inves-tigate law violations, not produce intelligence. The FBI reports directly to the Department of Justice (DOJ)—a highly politicized entity—and must establish the high standard of probable cause as part of the investigative approach to domestic security. If there's no viable case early on, as DOJ officials instruct, the scrutiny of a potential terrorist wastes resources. Dangerous men and women fall off watch lists, and more Americans live in fear, waiting for the next attack.

In the wake of attacks on American soil, from Orlando to San

Bernardino to Minnesota and New York City, it is clear the FBI's law enforcement approach is unable to disrupt enough fatal and dangerous attacks against our domestic targets before they happen.

We have to demand that the FBI stop lying to us. They go to the members of Congress, who don't know what questions to ask and just blow smoke. It would be refreshing if someone looked at FBI Director James Comey and said, "You guys might be working hard, but you're ineffective. The system isn't working and you aren't good at it." That's what I would say if given the chance.

After so many of the terror attacks just described, the FBI said that the terrorists were known to the agency. Well, if they were known to the FBI, the terrorists should've been stopped.

No one ever loses a job over these gross errors. I don't mean some agent—you can't drop it down to the lower levels of government. Who was alerted about the Phoenix memo in the FBI? We don't know their names. But I can guarantee that if something happens within the Milwaukee County Sheriff's Office, people say, "Sheriff Clarke let this happen" or "Sheriff Clarke did this." That's because I am accountable. And the FBI should be held accountable to the American public instead of operating in the dark shadows of anonymity.

3. Eliminate gun-free zones. Gun-free zones are killing fields.

As mass shootings continue to happen, some patterns are emerging from the after-action reports. I have seen several reports that point out why the assailant chose a location. It is a target rich for what the killer is trying to achieve: killing as many people as possible before being stopped. For that to occur, no other armed person can be nearby. The killer needs a gun-free zone.

In these cases, the incidents didn't end until the assailant killed himself or an armed officer or another armed person confronted him.

We may not be able to totally eliminate these mass shootings, but we can limit the carnage with a change of attitude about gun-free zones. Blame-the-gun advocates and proponents of gun-free zones hate to face these facts, but we need to have this discussion in the interest of sound public policy.

As the sheriff of a large urban county, I advise business establishments to take those *No Firearms* signs out of their windows and off the front door. Why? Malls and schools are notorious for bragging that they're gun-free zones, but those signs are providing intelligence to mass killers by sending this message: it will be a while before anyone can confront you, so this is a target-rich environment, especially if your end game is suicide-by-cop. Killers choose their locations, in part, because the people in the area are like grazing sheep, ill prepared for an attack by a hungry wolf.

Regardless, I'm not going to order private businesses to take down these gun-free zone signs. That's their choice. If a coffee place like Starbucks is a gun-free zone, I can buy coffee at a different location, I can brew coffee at home, or I can do without coffee that day. Though getting coffee is not a constitutional right, honoring the Second Amendment certainly is.

That's why public spaces controlled by government should *not* be gun-free zones. If I want to go to a park, a public facility, the courthouse, or a state college campus, that's a different story. I can't get a birth certificate anywhere but a courthouse. Kids going to college have to live and study on government-controlled college campuses. But we've had shootings in courthouses and college campuses. They are anything but airtight.

As unwise as it is for the government to disarm regular, law-abiding citizens, it's even worse that they disarm their law enforcement and military personnel. When the American government doesn't trust its own military to carry the firearms they have been trained to use, it's a sad day. It's infinitely worse when some goof like Nidal Hasan uses a gun among all those soldiers, and they have been stripped of their right to fight back. Or when people like Mohammad Abdulazeez and Abdulhakim Mujahid Muhammad drive by military recruitment centers because they know our soldiers are sitting ducks.

Why are gun-free zones on military bases? Every soldier knows how to use a weapon. When deployed, soldiers carry weapons at all times, even on the bases that practically guarantee they'll never encounter the enemy. According to the *Washington Post*, "current policy requires soldiers to register their own personal weapons with commanders and to keep those weapons in the arms room."[12] In other words, soldiers frequently would be safer if they were just walking down the street in their hometowns. This is a shame and a betrayal.

We cannot ignore or deny this any longer. Current public and business safety policy involving the prohibited carrying of firearms by law-abiding persons is too often designed from an emotional perspective and decades of conditioning that guns are evil. Guns are not evil. People are evil. Reasonable people would realize that only when a law-abiding person with a gun showed up did these mass killings end.

4. Quit planning for the last attack. After the marathon attack, Bostonians were understandably nervous when the race came around the following year. News sources reported that 3,500 police officers were deployed at the race, more than twice as many as usual, and spectators were asked not to bring backpacks. I don't blame Boston officials for these security restrictions, but their excessive caution demonstrated that they did not trust US intelligence capability. Thankfully, a terror attack did not occur again at the marathon, but not because of the doubling of officers and the installing of additional surveillance cameras.

Usually, terrorists do not strike in the same manner or location because they like to use the element of surprise.

Deploying a massive number of officers in an attempt to eliminate another intelligence failure is referred to as "planning for the last attack." We did this after 9/11 as well. Assigning seven thousand officers last year would not have prevented that act of war. Only better intelligence collection, analysis, and dissemination (sharing) reduce the likelihood of terror attacks.

These same types of intelligence failures contributed to the 9/11 attacks, and the reaction was the same: the government inconvenienced millions of American travelers at airports, suspected every American of terror involvement to the point of trampling on previously protected constitutional freedoms, and gave the federal government broad authority to encroach on privacy. In addition, Congress increased intelligence spending and created the Department of Homeland Security, one of the largest federal agencies, with a growing budget that had reached more than $60 billion per year in 2012.[13] In one of his rants, Dr. Ayman al-Zawahiri, spiritual leader of al-Qaeda, indicated that part of the objective of the 9/11 terror attack in the United States was to turn the American people against their government for intruding on their freedoms and to bankrupt our government with security spending. Mission accomplished. Even after this overreaction, two known terror suspects were able to board separate commercial airliners, one with a bomb in his underwear, and the other with a bomb in his shoe; Nidal Hasan was able to exchange e-mails with known terrorist and bomb-maker al-Awlaki before he massacred thirteen US soldiers and wounded thirty others. The FBI knew about this and did little with it.

The NSA and FBI have no problem, however, collecting and indefinitely storing the metadata of every law-abiding American citizen's cell phone calls, text messages, emails, credit card purchases, and web searches, claiming that it prevents terror attacks. These agencies were spying on Americans when the Tsarnaev brothers were planning their attack, but the brothers' actions didn't draw the attention of the FBI or NSA. The warning light was blinking red, but the watchmen were asleep at the switch.

Rather than inconvenience American citizens, the Boston Police Department should inconvenience the FBI and NSA by insisting that they do a better job of data collection, analysis, and information sharing. And, yes, they should profile terror suspects instead of spying on or suspecting every American of terror involvement.

Our only hope against terror is to stop taking it out on the American people after an attack, improve our national intelligence process, and hold people accountable when obvious failure occurs. (This is another thing that has not happened since 9/11—no one is held accountable.) Quality warning intelligence is a better model to more successfully detect, deter, disrupt, and mitigate terror attacks. It is a less costly approach not just in budgetary terms, but in safeguarding constitutional freedoms. We deserve privacy *and* security.

God forbid that a terror suspect straps explosives to his or her body and detonates them in a public space. The overreaction might be that the government makes every American citizen walk naked in public spaces to prevent the next attack.

5. Keep Terror-Related Criminals from Other Prisoners. Did you know that we are inadvertently creating a Petri dish of terrorism right here on American soil?

Holding terrorists in prisons gives them opportunities to convert others to their radical cause. Our prisons have become a terrorist recruiting network right under our noses. Instead, we should isolate terrorists from the general prison population to eliminate their access to a captive audience whom they can convert to their deathly cause. I'd ship these terrorists to Gitmo or create a different prison for them specifically. We must not allow them to try to radicalize our prisoners.

6. Have the Guts to Name the Enemy. Did you notice anything interesting about the assailants in these cases?

After all of these failures, the government refuses to address the elephant in the room—jihadism. In the case of the Fort Hood shooting, eyewitnesses say Hasan screamed, "Allahu Akbar!" as he shot the innocent. It means "God is great" and is the frequent cry of Islamic terrorists as they attack. (Some witnesses weren't familiar with this phrase, so they reproduced his words phonetically to investigators.) Would you believe that the official US Army report failed to mention Islam,[14] even though Hasan made his jihadist, religious motivations perfectly clear?

In the Pulse incident, a Muslim walked into a gay bar and mercilessly murdered forty-nine men and women. In the middle of his killing spree, he took a break to call 911 and a local television station to make sure everyone knew he'd pledged allegiance to ISIS. He also told cops that the Boston Tsarnaev brothers were his "homeboys." He allegedly took an online course with a radical, antigay imam. Yet somehow this incident was played out in the media in a way that put Christians in the crosshairs. CNN's Anderson Cooper notoriously interviewed Florida Attorney General Pam Bondi, who had expressed sympathy for the victims. In a remarkable display of willful ignorance, Cooper accused her of hypocrisy. After all, how could a person who opposed same-sex marriage also care if gay people are murdered in cold blood?

(Hey, Anderson Cooper, would you have asked President Obama the same thing had this slaughter occurred before Obama changed his stance on same-sex marriage? Or Mrs. Bill Clinton, who opposed gay marriage until five years ago? Doubtful. It staggers the mind that you had the gall to ask the question.)

American media and our political leaders are being purposefully obtuse when it comes to the topic of jihadism. We have to stop blaming each other and look squarely into the eyes of the enemy.

7. Do something meaningful. Contrary to countries like Great Britain, Russia, and Israel, where terrorism efforts are focused on monitoring without the burden of seeking a prosecution, the FBI continues to drop future terrorists from its radar screen at a time when we need to be more vigilant, not less. Outcry by the American people about such incidents falls on deaf ears. Accountability is nowhere to be found. A better approach is to create an agency solely dedicated to domestic intelligence—reducing the purview of the FBI and transferring these resources to an organization similar to MI5 in the United Kingdom.

It wouldn't be just another agency. We need to change the culture and mind-set of the FBI, and this culture change has to be made on the fly. ISIS will not give us a time-out to get our act together. Doing this will be tough since these agents have been trained to get evidence, establish probable cause, and prepare for an investigation. That's not intelligence work.

I met a twenty-year-old American citizen, who came from Pakistan, working at the Apple store.

"I applied for the Milwaukee Police Department," he told me as we stood next to rows of shiny new iPads. "I wanted to get into information technology, but they told me I had to start off being a beat cop and going through the police academy."

Eventually, he gave up and started working for Apple.

I looked at that eager-to-serve guy—a man with technology skills, who speaks two Arabic languages and knows the Pakistani culture and customs—and I thought, *I'd hire that guy in a second to do intelligence work.*

He didn't want to be a beat cop. He wanted to offer his analytical skills. And we should've let him do just that. After all, intelligence analysts ask these three questions:

1. Is this person a threat?
2. Does he have the means?
3. Is he planning an attack?

The guy in the Apple store didn't need a gun, arrest powers, or training about how to handcuff an arrestee to analyze that data. Our intelligence analysts should follow potential terrorists and never give up the observation until they're dead. He could have monitored credit card purchases, travel, and communication of potential terrorists. Even if one person on the watch list is quiet for six months, our analysts should know if he suddenly takes a flight to Yemen or Afghanistan. That behavior needs to trigger action so that our intelligence counterparts there can track him and keep an eye on him when he arrives and when he returns.

The FBI is still in a pre-9/11 mind-set in which the targets of an investigation are easily identified and arrest powers come in handy. In the United Kingdom's MI5 agency, analysts are not tasked with making arrests so they're focused on intelligence. The guy at the Apple store could've easily filled in a vitally important role, but our blinders prevented us from seeing his value.

No, we don't need another federal agency. We need a new mind-set that would approach terror in a way suited to the primary goal not of prosecution but of pre-emption and would reflect the new reality of our world, which is that terrorism is no longer only happening in a distant land. Instead, Americans, if not our bureaucrats, realize that the war has been brought to our soil, and it's time to stop being sitting ducks.

As a law enforcement administrator, I understand the complexities this type of effort requires. An independent entity, which reports directly to the White House, is the answer for both accountability and reliability.

We've done nothing to address the inadequate domestic intelligence functionality within our borders. This reprehensible lack of action requires a sober and forthright national conversation about the deficiencies that have allowed our flags to seem to fly perpetually at half-mast.

We require the proper organization and organizing mission that focus instead on identifying potential threats, establishing their capabilities, determining whether an attack is being planned, and alerting decision makers.

This organization does not exist in our country yet, but it needs to and soon. A new entity focused on protection, not prosecution, is the only way to protect Americans.

We live in a new era. Like it or not, the enemy is at war with us and has come to our home soil. This isn't the time to plant rose bushes and go about our daily lives. It's time to assess, adjust our protocol, and stand up for American lives.

President Obama has offered a pathetic, weak, and un-American solution: learn to live with it. Capitulating to hate and murderers is not acceptable to me, nor should it be to any American. It's up to the American people to demand that a new domestic security entity take up the protection of the homeland.

13

The TSA Is Whistling
Past the Graveyard

"WHAT DO YOU MEAN, I can't have more to drink?" a man called out drunkenly to a flight attendant on my way to New Hampshire. I'd hoped to use the two hours to my connecting flight in Charlotte to work on my iPad or possibly get some rest. But thirty-six-year-old Preston Bluntson had other plans for the passengers.[1] "I already paid for one," he said, apparently too inebriated to know that he had not paid for one.

That's the G-rated version of what he said because every sentence involved throwing F-bombs and other four-letter words. I kept my eyes on him as he switched seats and continued to hurl expletives around the cabin. He was acting as though the airplane was his private jet. The other passengers seemed intimidated by the man's obnoxious behavior, but I had no handcuffs to secure him if he got so out of hand that early into the flight he needed to be restrained. I didn't want to be grappling with this guy for the entire two-hour flight. Instead, I planned and waited until the perfect moment before making a move.

In one exchange with the flight attendant he was so belligerent that I had to leave my seat to intervene. "Are you okay?" I asked the flight attendant. He indicated that my intervening should be enough to settle him down. I turned to Bluntson. He wanted another drink.

"You need to chill out. It's not worth it."

He stopped, sensing I wasn't playing around. I returned to my seat, but his restraint didn't last long. I motioned to the flight attendant to come back to me, and I asked that the airport be radioed so Charlotte police officers could meet me at the gate. I watched the flight attendant pick up the phone and talk. I'm sure it's required for the attendant to notify the flight deck when a problem arises in the cabin.

As soon as the wheels touched down with the plane still moving fast on the runway, the goof immediately got out of his seat and stood up. The flight attendant told him to return to his seat, but he continued to be loud and profane.

While the plane taxied to the gate, he started taunting me. "Hey, everyone, that's Sheriff Clarke over there," he yelled. He looked back at me and said, "What are you going to do about it?" Again, his statements were peppered with more four-letter words. "What is he going to do about it?"

When he refused to sit down, I quickly got out of my seat, walked toward Bluntson, and ordered him to sit down. I was loaded for bear. Every passenger and the flight attendant had to put up with his actions for two hours. Now it was our turn to show him how we felt about it. When he refused to take my directive, I shoved him facedown, pinned him across two seats, and used my weight to hold him in that position with one arm behind his back.

"Stay there," I commanded. "Stop resisting. If you don't, things will not turn out well for you."

"Oh, you're one of those kind of n—." He continued to struggle, but he wasn't getting up from the position I had him in. If he had, I was willing to apply a higher level of physical force. He wasn't going anywhere.

I held him there and looked around the cabin while he ranted about my supporting Donald Trump. Could this have been a distraction for something more troublesome than a stupid drunk? I looked up and down the aisle of the plane. Nothing looked suspicious other than that I was physically restraining this goof. Not a passenger moved.

I held him until we arrived safely at our terminal. A uniformed officer boarded the plane, and the flight attendant conveyed information.

"Officer, over here," I yelled. "Give me your handcuffs!"

I did not want to let go of the advantage I had with the positioning. The officer gave me her handcuffs. I got one cuff on and told him to put the other arm behind his back. For the first time in that entire two-hour flight, he complied. I cuffed the other wrist, got off him, and the police sergeant took control of him. More officers had arrived. By that time, I wasn't worried about jurisdiction or any of that other nonsense. I was worried only about protecting people. It was instinctive. It's what I have been doing for close to four decades. It was second nature.

The airport police escorted him off the plane. Off the jetway and inside the terminal, he continued to be loud and profane toward the officers and airport personnel. They got a look at what we on that flight had endured.

He was charged with several state misdemeanors and was bailed out the following night. Such incidents should be charged as federal statute violations and reviewed by the US Attorney's Office to send a message of deterrence to passengers about interfering with flight crews and intimidating passengers. Also, where were the federal air marshals on board to take control of the situation?

"In all my years flying, I've never seen anything like it," one passenger said. "The sheriff handled himself extremely well. It could have gotten a lot worse because the guy was not backing down."

People turned to social media to praise my actions and even called me a "black Chuck Norris."

Where Have All the Air Marshals Gone?

While I appreciate the encouraging words, I'd much rather the government put more resources toward security when a flight is in the air. All the security is on the ground. The 9/11 hijackers waited to strike until after they boarded the plane. Airplane passengers now are hostage to an unruly passenger. Flights have had to make emergency landings and be diverted for similar incidents. We shouldn't be forced to choose between traveling and being safe. In 2008, CNN did a nationwide investigation and discovered that fewer than 1 percent of flights in the United States have an armed federal air marshal on board.[2] Rational Americans would recognize that not all of the nation's daily flights will be protected, but you'd think the percentage would be higher than one measly percent. Especially since that year alone, the Federal Air Marshal Service (FAMS) was given $720 million.[3] Where did the money go?

In 2014, *USA Today* quoted John Casaretti, national president of the Air Marshal Association/CWA, on how many FAMs are on planes. "There are around 30,000 commercial flights per day over the U.S.," said Casaretti. "If you were to attempt to place a team of just two FAMs on each flight, it would require an agency of over 75,000 FAMs (accounting for training and days off). FAMs cover a very small percentage of commercial flights." How about something as simple as allowing off-duty law enforcement officers after alerting the airline and the Transportation Security Administration (TSA) that they are traveling armed to board with their firearm? How much would that cost? Nothing, but the TSA doesn't trust local police.

It makes sense why the TSA won't settle the speculation on how many air marshals exist, but Michael D. Pascarella, assistant supervisory air marshal in charge of the Public Affairs Office of the TSA, acknowledged there were only "thousands."

Former Navy SEAL Clay Biles, a federal air marshal for five years and the author of the book *Unsecure Skies*, told *USA Today*, he estimates there are 3,300 FAMs. However, 34 percent of them are stuck on the ground doing management, operations, or training work. Biles said,

> We call them "chair marshals," riding out their career in management . . . That leaves 66% of the workforce to perform in-flight security duties. If one accounts for vacations, sick leave, medical leave and days off, some air marshals working in operations have told me that this accounts for less than one half percent of all U.S.-flagged aircraft being covered by federal air marshals.[4]

When Tom Coburn was the ranking Republican on the Homeland Security and Governmental Affairs Committee in 2015, the Oklahoma senator said the TSA budget had gone up despite the dwindling number of agents. He said, "it is unclear to what extent the FAMs program is reducing risk to aviation security, despite the more than $820 million annually that is spent on the program."[5]

Apparently, agents have fled the air marshal service because they believe the agency puts its agents in danger. "Everything they did set us up to get murdered," Richard Vasquez, a former marshal who left the program in January 2015, told *National Review*. He said the biggest issue was that the agency was not trying to help them be covert at all. They had agents carrying guns that were too big to be concealed. He revealed that on some international flights, the government forced the agents to board the plane first as if the other passengers wouldn't notice the guy with the gun and no luggage sitting on the plane.

"The numbers are dwindling; now they're not telling the public this, but that's the fact," Vasquez said. "The only people who aren't trying to leave are people who are past that age-37 range and are meaning to retire."

That's comforting, isn't it? No. The federal government is whistling past the graveyard, hoping we don't see what is plainly before our eyes.

But safety precautions need to occur way before we end up thirty thousand feet in the air. How many times have you been harassed or inconvenienced at the airport before you even board? I've experienced much of this when trying to check my firearm at Reagan International Airport.

"We found this," a TSA agent said to me once, holding up a loose bullet. He had the look of a teacher who'd just found a cheat sheet stuck in my shoe.

"I know," I explained as I stood next to the counter. When you check your weapon before a flight, you have to wait off to the side. It's not a big deal, but it's a hassle. Some days are worse than others.

"Yes, that's just a bullet." The magazine for the gun I was checking was in the same pouch. The magazine for my weapon takes nine bullets. To increase the capability to ten, I chamber a round, then slide another one into the magazine. "When I checked my weapon, it has to be unloaded. I put the loose bullet in a pouch with the magazine attached to the bag like I always do."

"You can't have loose bullets," he said. "So we're keeping this."

"Take it," I said. "Fine." It was just one freaking bullet, but it represented a lot more. Government "box-checking" at the expense of Americans' safety. No discretion is allowed. On another occasion, with a different carrier, I was standing off to the side waiting for them to evaluate my weapon, and they came back with my magazine.

As part of the check-in procedure the ticket agent took me through a series of required questions. She asked if the bullets were out of the magazine and in a box. I said no. Now I have been traveling frequently for the last two years. I had never been told the bullets had to be out of the magazine. What are they worried about? The firearm will be in the cargo portion and inaccessible to me or anybody else.

She found an ammo box for me to use, but I fumed. As I took the bullets out of the magazine one by one, I thought, *This is so stupid. What difference does it make if they're in a box or not since the weapon is in the cargo section? It didn't make a difference on Delta, United, or Southwest, but suddenly it's a big deal on American Airlines?*

Once I was at LAX with paperwork allowing me to board armed as law enforcement.

"Sorry, sir," the TSA lady said. "You can take your gun but not your knife."

"Why?" I asked.

"Only Border Patrol can take knives on an airplane."

"Why not a law enforcement officer who is already carrying a gun?"

"We're just following the rules, sir."

I took my knife back down to the ticket agent, explained my situation, and showed my badge and credentials. I really didn't want to lose my knife.

"Give me the knife," the ticket agent said after he examined my papers. "I'll put it in your checked bag."

I found that promise dubious since my bag had already gone through screening. I figured he just wanted to get rid of me.

However, the guy overrode the screening. Although that is problematic, the guy used sound discretion and did not endanger air travel. The TSA people at the checkpoint could have done the same thing by letting me on with the knife *and* my gun after checking my law enforcement credentials, but a follow-the-rules mentality reigned that day.

When I got home, the knife was in my garment bag.

Why doesn't the government allow sound discretion?

I travel to Mexico or the Caribbean every year. Once, returning from Mexico, I landed in the Atlanta airport. Though I'd already been screened in Mexico and was apparently not a threat to board an international flight, I arrived in America to be screened again. They took us from a sterile area, where we'd already been searched, through a nonsterile area to get to the connecting flight to come back to Milwaukee. That meant we had to be screened again.

"Why are you taking passengers who've already been screened through this process again?" I asked.

I already knew the answer: they had an architecture problem. Because of their setup, they couldn't make sure screened passengers stay screened.

"You're in a nonsterile area now," he said, "so we have to screen you again."

"I was screened in Mexico," I said, then I commented, "This is the problem. We don't focus on the real threat."

"Americans can be terrorists too. I'm just following the rules," he said curtly.

I'm not given to anger, but my blood started to boil. Why would he want to insult an American citizen like that? Sure, Americans can be radicalized, but most of us are not. This agent wanted to paint all

Americans with a broad brush. You do that with Muslims and you are an Islamophobe, with African Americans and you're a racist. But it's perfectly acceptable to insult an entire nation of US citizens not suspected of terrorism?

I was about to give the guy a two-word suggestion, when my wife came closer to me and said quietly, "Come on, David, let's go."

I held my tongue. I didn't need to be arrested to rebuke the guy for his mind-set that all Americans are potential terrorists. But his sentence is the main problem facing safety on airline flights across America. The federal government wastes time and resources by focusing on a sheriff instead of someone like Omar Mateen. People like me don't need additional screening. They knew I was a sheriff because I had my badge right there in my bag. What is the risk of the sheriff of Milwaukee boarding a plane and shooting it up? Sure, it's possible, but what is the likelihood?

Life has risks, so there's no zero-risk plan of action. That's why we need a risk-based model, not a follow-the-rules model. Washington, DC, operates under a rules-based instead of risk-based model. Theirs is a check-the-box mentality that undermines Americans' faith in the government. We shouldn't give up or change our way of life, like at airports, to protect a failing bureaucratic system or because we are afraid of truly taking on an enemy intent on destroying Western culture.

Why do we still have to take our shoes off during TSA screening?

It's been years since shoe-bomber Richard Reid tried to detonate his shoes. In 2001, he literally did everything but wear a nametag indicating that he was a terrorist: He got a British passport in Belgium, flew to Paris, and used cash to buy a one-way ticket to Florida. Then he went to the airport without any luggage for an international flight. On that day, three airports failed to pick up these enormous clues. Yet the American government decided to "fix it" by telling all Americans to take off their shoes when they go through airport security.

Later, a Nigerian man named Umar Farouk Abdulmutallab hid plastic explosives in his underwear on a flight from Amsterdam to Detroit. Here's what you *don't* know about Abdulmutallab. His dad called the U.S. Embassy a month before the incident and said his son had called to tell him that was the last time his father would ever hear from him. His father feared his son might do something drastic, so he called the embassy. What did they do with this information? Nothing. When Abdulmutallab showed up and bought a ticket with three thousand dollars cash, no one asked him anything.

Once again, we had an intelligence failure. Yet because of this underwear bomber, millions of Americans have their privacy invaded by full body scans. Again, we miss the flashing red lights. Do we really want the government to see us naked as a precondition of getting on a flight? Do we really want to hobble through security check points without shoes? I like to wear cowboy boots, and I can tell you it's not easy to get through the check points while wearing them.

Let's Keep Our Senses . . . and Our Shoes

I think the answer of most Americans is this: "I don't want it, but if it makes us safer, I'm willing to put up with it."

But what if I told you it doesn't make us safer?

Technology Band-Aids can't take the place of intelligence. Israel, for example, has the most airtight security, even though Israelis are the target of much anti-Semitic hatred. They've never had the no-shoes policy and never suffered an act of terror.

Yet here in America, we are herded through long security lines while TSA agents bark orders at us. "Get everything out of your pockets. Put your laptop in a separate bin." These ineffective tactics all over America cost airlines millions of dollars of missed flights, not to mention much angst and embarrassment for Americans. It's undignified and unsanitary for a grown man to be forced to wrangle off his shoes in a line of other people, then walk on the dirty floor that thousands of others have walked down with their bare feet over the previous hours. Then when belongings finally come out of the X-ray machine, one has to grab the shoes, belt, and watch from the conveyor belt, and try to hurriedly put everything back on before the other bins push them down to the end of the line. It's annoying, unnecessary, invasive, and another sign of government incompetence.

Wouldn't it be earth shattering if someone in Washington, DC, did a risk assessment by studying other nations that allow passengers to keep their shoes on? What if, after looking at the information, bureaucrats said, "Listen, we were wrong. Everyone can keep their shoes on during airport security checkpoints"?

But that's not how our government works. Once something is in place—no matter how ineffective—no one has the guts to be the guy who says, "Enough!" It takes a small amount of courage to unring the bell, but it's still more than our politicians seem to possess. They don't want to take the chance that something might happen somewhere.

Real leaders, however, can evaluate the risk, realize that something somewhere might happen, and have the courage to change the policy anyway.

In his final report to Congress, Senator Coburn wrote that "there is and always will be a perpetual struggle between security and liberty in a free society. Liberty requires security, but too much security can result in a loss of liberty. And the erosion of freedoms is rarely restored. We should never have to give up our rights to preserve them, and our

Constitution which specifies the rights of the people and the limitations of the government does not even allow for such an exchange. This balancing act has become increasingly complicated."

I agree.

We're harassing Americans unnecessarily because we're focusing on everyone instead of the more probable terrorists, we're ignoring actual intelligence, and we seem to seriously lack common sense.

It's time the TSA realizes these regulations are stupid, don't stop terror attacks, and hurt Americans every day.

Let's give these policies—and maybe even the bureaucrats—the boot.

14

The Left's Dreaded Enemy: Black Conservatives

I REACHED FOR A MUG in my office, passing over the one with the word *Cowboy* on it and settling on the one emblazoned with John Wayne's profile. The words inside the rim—*Courage is being scared but saddling up anyway*—disappeared under my coffee, half & half, and Truvia.

"Dear David . . ." I read the first e-mail in my long list and sighed. I'm not a *sit*-in-the-office sheriff because there are very few problems in my office. The problems lurk out there in the field. I physically go to the office only if administrative things need work like signatures on forms, my e-mail needs to be checked, and other administrative tasks need my attention—necessary evils that keep me from being on the street. "I couldn't even bring myself to call you Mr. Clarke," I continued reading. "You are a sorry excuse for a man, an African American man at that. You are a white washed piece of . . . I watched your interview . . . on FOX, and almost punched a hole through my TV. Who raised your coon . . . ?"

That'll wake you up.

"You are a disgrace to the Milwaukee Police Department," it continued, "a white stain on the black community. You can believe that your white friends and colleagues are your friends if you want to, but they won't hesitate to shoot down your 17 year old grandson or slam your 28 year old niece's head into the ground. You think that because the white man wears blue, you can wear blue and be accepted. You're a joke. To them, behind your back, YOU ARE JUST ANOTHER N—. A house n— at that."

The fan mail was signed, "a member of the African American community."

Believe it or not, that was the edited version.

I took a sip of my coffee and smiled.

Know what I call it when I get a really offensive e-mail accusing me of selling out my race? Tuesday.

"How do you read those types of e-mails without getting down on yourself?" one coworker asked when he walked by my desk and saw me grinning. It's easy. I know my identity doesn't rest in outboxes of "fans" like these.

Let's face it.

It's very easy to get "identity" wrong. Frequently, we identify ourselves by the color of our skin (even though Martin Luther King Jr. warned against that very approach). We might identify ourselves by our accomplishments . . . or, more likely, our failures. We might define ourselves by the fact that we have a wonderful spouse or great kids. We might rely very heavily on the label we give ourselves, Democrat or Republican, and fight with anyone who isn't in our group. But when you define yourself by anything other than the way God defines you, you'll get in trouble. Only God can really define you. You can't find yourself by going on a spiritual retreat, practicing yoga, or looking deeply into your soul.

Your self-worth has to be based on more than trends, popularity, or other people's opinions.

A lack of self-worth is one of the most pressing problems in the inner cities today. Note that I didn't say "self-confidence." I think we might have way too much of that. (Did you know that social scientists have determined that incarcerated prisoners have the most self-confidence of any other group? The worlds tells us that self-confidence will solve a host of problems. But the prisoners, so full of it, tell a different tale.) Self-confidence just isn't enough.

Politically Orphaned

I am a man of God. I always carry a prayer book, I keep a Bible in my truck, and I pray every day. I certainly won't let raving idiots typing out diatribes in their mothers' basements affect the way I view myself. Hate mail like this happens so regularly that I pay little attention to it. I'm sharing a couple of these e-mails so you can more adequately understand what it's like to be a black conservative in America today.

Here's another:

> You are the definition of an apologist and a House negro. Coons like yourself are the reason the black race is in the position we are presently. I feel so sorry for the blacks in your county. They don't stand a chance against police misconduct. You, sir, are a Grade A piece of . . . When you are laid to rest, I hope your soul burns in the bottom pits of hell.

Most people assume being a black American conservative is like being any other conservative. After all, we believe in limited government and low taxes through a restrained federal bureaucracy; we believe the Constitution protects individuals, not groups; we believe a strong national defense and safe streets are critical to liberty, freedom, and an orderly society; we believe in states' rights; and we frequently believe in a Higher Power.

That, however, is where the similarities end.

To be a black conservative in America is to be orphaned personally and politically by the Left. That's because the Left wants us to be set apart, be pushed out of the nest, or perhaps earn our own entry in the *Guinness Book of World Records* . . . right next to the lady with the largest collection of garden gnomes or the world's fattest twins. We are—they would have you believe—abnormal. Even "traitors to our race," as my admirer above mentioned. We *could* accurately be labeled as "independent thinkers," since we're not taking our marching orders from anyone but ourselves. Instead, we're called "Uncle Toms" and "sellouts." Oh, and everything we do or say—without exception—is attributed to us trying to gain acceptance from white conservatives.

As if we aren't capable of independent thought.

Being black *and* conservative is such an odd combination that we need a new classification. Don't believe me? Take a look around the world of politics. Sarah Palin is not a "female conservative." She's just "conservative." Rush Limbaugh is not a "white male conservative." He's just "conservative." But Supreme Court Justice Clarence Thomas, Dr. Ben Carson, economist Thomas Sowell, four-star general Colin Powell, and former US Secretary of State Condoleezza Rice belong to a rare class. They belong to a special category of people so unique that their oddity can't be contained in one word. These people are never described simply as "conservatives." They are "black conservatives"—no matter what else they accomplish with their lives. By adding the descriptor "black," the Left wants you to begin to think of the phrase "black conservatives" as an oxymoron . . . words that are apparently contradictory appearing together: "jumbo shrimp," "pretty ugly," "living dead."

That's because the Left demands black conservatives' political and personal beliefs become their cultural identity. Did you know that Clarence Thomas was once associated with the Black Panthers? Yep. But the moment he began to think more conservatively, he became a traitor to his race for not being "black enough." Got it? Here's a helpful guide:

Blackness ≠ having black skin.

Blackness = swallowing Democrat policies whole.

You can be called "black," even if you're white. That's how important the Left believes regurgitating Democrat talking points is. We saw this in 1998 when Nobel Laureate Toni Morrison (who's black) called Bill Clinton (who's white) the "first black president." Why on earth would she describe him that way? She explained: "Clinton displays almost every trope of blackness: single-parent household, born poor, working-class, saxophone-playing, McDonald's-and-junk-food-loving boy from Arkansas." In other words, Clinton was the first "black president" because of a string of negative racial stereotypes. (Imagine for one second the racial hysteria that would've ensued had Rush Limbaugh called Clinton "black" based on the fact that he liked to eat cheap food and was poor.)

My point is this: "blackness" is a status the Left awards *and* revokes.

Or at least, phony self-serving plantation gate-keeping liberals *try* to award and revoke it.

They go after those who don't walk lockstep with them, seeing them as runaway slaves. The resulting smear campaign is a modern metaphorical lynching.

Which other ethnic group endures this politically?

None.

My Badge of Honor

But here's a message to "a member of the African American community" and others who try to intimidate me: I don't care what you think, so your approval or rejection doesn't matter to me. As I mentioned, I'm not defined by your opinion or my popularity. Because my identity rests in God alone, you can't touch me.

My faith in God also allows me to speak the truth, so get ready for it. The cultural gate keepers of blackness—people like Jesse Jackson and Al Sharpton—have ruined more black minds with their support of a culture of dependency than crack cocaine and whiskey. They have convinced too many blacks that perpetual victimhood is the only source of their power. They've made careers out of creating and prolonging turmoil between blacks and whites, which keeps blacks enslaved in resentment. They could criticize me all day every day—and some do!—and their ill-conceived, petty insults are a badge of honor. The *only* membership card that has any value to me is the one that guarantees me all the rights and privileges afforded by the US Constitution as a citizen of the United States. My rights are inalienable, irrevocable.

And I plan to use every last one of them.

This book is my effort to exercise my First Amendment right to free speech. No matter how many hate-filled, racist e-mails I receive, I will never shut up. I want my fellow black brothers and sisters to start thinking for themselves, to break free from the shackles that white liberals have placed on them. It's time to shake things up. The black vote has been the most reliably Democratic voting bloc for the past thirty years, so much so that the Democratic Party takes us for granted.

Here are the rather shocking numbers. In 1976, 83 percent of black voters cast their vote for Jimmy Carter; in 1980, that percentage was repeated. In 1984, Walter Mondale got 91 percent of black voters' ballots; in 1988, Michael Dukakis received 89 percent; in 1992, Clinton

got 83 percent and then 84 percent four years later. Al Gore got 90 percent in 2000; John Kerry got 88 percent in 2004. Then, when blacks
had the chance to vote for the first (actually) black candidate, they
came out in droves. In 2008 and 2012, blacks voted for Barack Obama
95 percent and 93 percent, respectively.[1]

What other demographic votes that way and higher every election
cycle? None do. That means Democrat politicians no longer even have
to try to win our votes. They had us as at hello, and they know it.
ESPN personality Stephen A. Smith (who's black) believes this high
level of loyalty to Democrats is damaging to blacks. Here's what he told
a crowd at Vanderbilt University:

> What I dream is that for one election, just one, every black per-
> son in America vote Republican . . . Black folks in America are
> telling one party, "We don't [care] about you." They're telling the
> other party, "You've got our vote." Therefore, you have labeled
> yourself "disenfranchised" because one party knows they've got
> you under their thumb. The other party knows they'll never
> get you and nobody comes to address your interest.[2]

While I applaud Smith's idea of shocking the Democratic Party
by essentially shopping around politically, we need more than a one-
election gimmick. We need to recognize that the destructive liberal
ideology of Democrats has destroyed the black family, destroyed
black motivation, destroyed the once strong black work ethic, and
estranged black men from involvement in their children's lives.
We need to force the members of the Democratic Party to come to
terms with what they've done—and continue to do—to their most
loyal friends.

Sadly, this damage was predicted and could've been prevented.

Turns Out Families Do Matter

Here's what happened five decades ago that could've made the difference. In the mid-1960s, Lyndon B. Johnson declared an "unconditional war" on poverty. In his 1964 State of the Union, he said, "Our aim is not only to relieve the symptoms of poverty, but to cure it and, above all, to prevent it."

Sounds good, right?

Johnson asked Daniel Patrick Moynihan—who, at the time, was assistant secretary of labor—to help develop programs that could assist in poverty reduction in inner cities.

Moynihan noticed a very unusual pattern as he sorted through the statistics relating to poor people. In the past, black male unemployment and welfare enrollment always went together in a predictable pattern. If unemployment went up, welfare enrollment went up. People assumed that if a black male had a job, the women and children in his household would reap the financial benefits as well. As Moynihan reviewed the charts, however, he realized this correlation no longer existed. Even as more and more black men landed jobs, more and more black women enrolled in welfare.

That was a real head scratcher. Moynihan and his team dived headfirst into the numbers and learned, first, that the number of single-parent families was growing in the ghetto. No one could argue that. As more and more men left their families—creating matriarchal families—males became alienated.

Moynihan reported that single moms frequently got pregnant by multiple partners and rarely managed to "shape their children's character and ability" in ways that allowed them to become prosperous citizens.

Families, he said, "shape their children's character and ability. By and large, adult conduct in society is learned as a child." When the family unit is broken, the children learn bad behavior from the adults: not to finish school, not to remain unemployed, not to take care of children they had fathered, and not to obey the law. By living with married parents, kids learn common beneficial virtues that encourage looking beyond just surviving the moment. Husbands and wives who were committed to each other planned for the future, saved money, and helped their children plan for their futures.

In other words, families matter. It was a chilling realization as the family in the inner cities dwindled. Kay S. Hymowitz wrote about the Moynihan report, "Separate and unequal families, in other words, meant that blacks would have their liberty, but that they would be strangers to equality. Hence Moynihan's conclusion: 'a national effort towards the problems of Negro Americans must be directed towards the question of family structure.'"[3]

Miraculously, President Johnson took to heart this research. In a speech to Howard University, he used language from Moynihan's unpublished report by saying it was time for "the next and more profound stage of the battle for civil rights." He said "the breakdown of the Negro family structure" was "the consequence of ancient brutality, past injustice and present prejudice." He added, "When the family collapses, it is the children that are usually damaged. When it happens on a massive scale, the community itself is crippled."

How did America respond?

In August 1965, the Moynihan report was leaked to *Newsweek*. It just so happened that a few days after the magazine ran the story, the national conversation on race would change perhaps forever. On August 11, a Los Angeles black woman was pulled over by a white policeman for suspicion of driving while intoxicated. The crowds who'd gathered to watch the interaction broke into violence. Six days of riots resulted in thirty-four deaths, more than one thousand injured people, $40 million worth of property damage, and nearly four thousand arrests.

The riots, which took place in a poor black neighborhood in South Central Los Angeles called Watts, perplexed Americans. Why would black people burn down their own community? As the violence unfolded on their television screens, Americans were less ready to accept Moynihan's explanation of life in the ghetto. They wondered whether President Johnson was trying to explain away the riots with this report. The civil rights leaders weren't buying the results of the report either. They wanted to portray the riots as the result of white injustice and prejudice, not the systematic breakdown of the family.

The executive director of the National Urban League strongly spoke out against Moynihan's report. Family is a "peripheral issue. The problem is discrimination," he said. The NAACP published criticism of the report, saying it was a "highly sophomoric treatment of illegitimacy." Blacks were no more "promiscuous" than their wealthier white counterparts, who had greater access to contraception, abortion, and adoption. But the biggest criticism, the one that stuck, was this: Moynihan's report "blamed the victim."

No one, of course, wants to "blame the victim."

After the poor reception of the Moynihan report, Johnson changed course, creating government programs to help subsidize the lives of poor Americans at great cost. Even though he created welfare, Medicaid, and food stamp programs to help eradicate poverty, his programs had the opposite effect.

Here's why.

Imagine that you were a single mom getting benefits from the federal government. You'd get more money by being single than by having a husband who managed to hold down a job. If you got married, the need-based benefits would go down drastically. Single moms received fewer services if their family's income rose, so they (quite rationally) made the decision to keep the federal government's provisions. That marginalized black unwed fathers, making them feel less than useless. Also, it separated marriage from children. In the past, the old playground taunt was more or less sequentially true: First comes love, then comes marriage, then comes so-and-so with a baby carriage. With the new programs, mothers were less likely to marry the fathers of their children so they could keep the federal benefits.

The Heritage Foundation put it this way:

The War on Poverty crippled marriage in low-income communities. As means-tested benefits were expanded, welfare began to serve as a substitute for a husband in the home, eroding marriage among lower-income Americans. In addition, the welfare system actively penalized low-income couples who did marry by eliminating or substantially reducing benefits. As husbands left the home, the need for more welfare to support single mothers increased. The War on Poverty created a destructive feedback loop: Welfare promoted the decline of marriage, which generated the need for more welfare.

Today, unwed childbearing and the resulting growth of single-parent homes is the most important cause of official child poverty. If poor women who give birth outside of marriage were married to the fathers of their children, two-thirds would immediately be lifted out of official poverty and into self-sufficiency.[4]

The liberal War on Poverty turned out to be basically a declaration of war on the black family. As the government expanded, it gave handouts that discouraged self-improvement, employment, and marriage.

Even though Johnson described his War on Poverty as an "investment" that would make "taxpayers out of taxeaters"[5] and "return its cost manifold to the entire economy," it didn't turn out that way.

Project 21's Derryck Green wrote about the effect of Johnson's War on Poverty on black Americans:

The disastrous effects of the government's management of anti-poverty initiatives are recognizable across racial lines, but the destruction is particularly evident in the black community. It effectively subsidized the dissolution of the black family by rendering the black man's role as a husband and a father irrelevant, invisible and—more specifically—disposable. The result has been several generations of blacks born into broken homes and broken communities experiencing social, moral and economic chaos. It fosters an inescapable dependency that primarily, and oftentimes solely, relies on government to sustain livelihoods.[6]

Robert Rector, writing in the *Wall Street Journal*, called Johnson's War on Poverty a catastrophe:

The federal government currently runs more than 80 means-tested welfare programs that provide cash, food, housing, medical care and targeted social services to poor and low-income Americans. Government spent $916 billion on these programs in 2012 alone, and roughly 100 million Americans received aid from at least one of them, at an average cost of $9,000 per recipient. (That figure doesn't include Social Security or Medicare benefits.) Federal and state welfare spending, adjusted for inflation, is 16 times greater than it was in 1964. If converted to cash, current means-tested spending is five times the amount needed to eliminate all official poverty in the U.S.

LBJ promised that the war on poverty would be an "investment" that would "return its cost manifold to the entire economy." But the country has invested $20.7 trillion in 2011 dollars over the past 50 years. What does America have to show for its investment? Apparently, almost nothing: The official poverty rate persists with little improvement.[7]

Twenty-eight months after the report was published, Moynihan could see that LBJ had missed an opportunity to really address the underlying issues. He stated, "It appears that the nation may be in the process of reproducing the tragic events of the Reconstruction, giving to Negroes the forms of legal equality, but withholding the economic and political resources which are the bases of social equality."[8]

By the way, Moynihan wrote his report when only 25 percent of black children grew up in homes without fathers. Though that number is way too high, Moynihan predicted that the number would skyrocket. Tragically, he was correct. Now, 70 percent of black children are growing up without dads in the home, the rate of pregnancy among unwed black females is more than twice as high as the rate among white females, schools are failing, and there are high black unemployment and obscene rates of poverty and criminal involvement.

This is what real racism looks like.

Financially discouraging marriage and encouraging black people to rely on government handouts undermined the traditional mores of blacks. Frederick Douglass, Booker T. Washington, and W. E. B. DuBois agreed that black people had to grab opportunity by the throat. No mention was made of relying on the government. These three believed that anyone who didn't advance the idea of self-reliance was no friend of the black man in America. By the race-hustling crowd definition, Douglass, Washington, and DuBois would be the original black conservative "sellouts" and "Uncle Toms." I'm sure they would be getting hateful e-mails if they lived today.

And check out what Malcolm X had to say about self-reliance:

The American black man should be focusing his every effort toward building his own businesses and decent homes for himself. As other ethnic groups have done, let the black people, wherever possible, however possible, patronize their own kind, hire their own kind, and start in those ways to build up the black race's ability to do for itself. That's the only way the American black man is ever going to get respect.[9]

That's a far cry from the food stamp and welfare mentality that the liberal Democrats have inculcated into the black culture.

When I was first entering politics and trying to decide which party to align with, I hesitated. Why do we have to be so partisan? I feel that hyperpartisanship is part of the problem in America. But I decided to run as a Democrat, and I'm not willing to voluntarily leave the party. My mom and dad raised their kids to believe in God, recite the Pledge of Allegiance, embrace education, and accept responsibility for our actions. My parents raised me with a lot of loving guidance and provided a foundation of values like hard work, self-confidence, and knowing how to get up after falling down. They taught me that the key to succeeding in an unfair world was for black people to be doubly prepared to compete. My parents would not stand for us children blaming white people for our problems, or believing that the color of our skin would prevent us from succeeding. My parents didn't see these values as conservative per se. They traditionally voted for Democrats.

Though my great-grandmother always voted Republican, my parents were Truman Democrats, Jack Kennedy Democrats, and Bobby Kennedy Democrats, not Nancy Pelosi or Harry Reid Democrats.

Because the Democratic Party has traditionally been comprised of self-reliant, hardworking individuals, I will not give it up to a bunch of white liberals like Pelosi and Mrs. Bill Clinton who push policies that hurt black Americans. Those left-wingers are scared to death that a black conservative voice, a voice like mine, might start to resonate with other Democrats. That's why they try to discredit me, to stigmatize me, to unceremoniously push me out of the party. My principles have not changed one bit over my lifetime, but liberal Democratic Party principles have gone off the rails. Everything about the Democratic Party has changed. (Would John F. Kennedy be welcomed today as a Democrat?) Liberals like to call themselves progressive. The only thing that they are progressing is black people's misery.

I'm not going anywhere. Supreme Court Justice Clarence Thomas tells a great anecdote about the former prime minister of England. Someone asked Winston Churchill why he became prime minister. He responded, "Ambition." Then he was asked why he stayed so long, and he replied, "Anger."

That's how I feel about the Democratic Party. I'm not letting it get away with this political genocide of black people; I'm staying to free black minds from the shackles of the destructive ideology of modern liberalism.

Racism Is Not Rampant

If you're a black person reading this book, please take a stand and fight with me to reform the Democratic Party from within.

If you're a white Republican reading this book, fight with me too.

It's as much your fight as it is mine to help me beat back the black gatekeepers who have been given license by white liberal Democrats to metaphorically lynch me.

America's not perfect. But it still offers every American black or otherwise who is willing to work hard the best chance of experiencing our full potential as human beings. Is everything in America fair? Of course not. Do racism and discrimination still exist? Sure they do. This is all a part of the imperfection of the human condition. But in 2017, racism is episodic, not rampant or institutional. The challenge is to work for a better future without being fixated on the ugly scars of the past.

Twenty-first-century blacks need to call for a truce when it comes to fighting the slavery of our ancestors generations ago so that we can focus on taking advantage of everything that America offers us today: raising and educating our children, owning a home, building wealth, and being free to pursue a life of our choosing.

I've made my peace with America and have decided to move on.

I'm moving on as an American, a Democrat, a man of God, and a sovereign human being, no matter what the personal or political cost may be. I am a public servant. It is not about me anymore. It is about the next generation.

15

Convention of States:
The Next American Revolution

AFTER I WAS APPOINTED Milwaukee County sheriff, then won my first election, I had the chance to run for mayor. People told me, "You've got to do it for the city. It's got to be you."

When I talked to my wife, Julie, about it, she wasn't too thrilled. Being the sport that she is, however, she said she'd support my decision. Ultimately, I made the wrong call: I ran. It was too soon. I had just been elected to my first office, and now I was thinking about running a large city.

After I made my announcement, my political strategist and fund-raiser—the very people who had encouraged me to run—abandoned me. The Democratic Party came after them and said that if they helped me, they'd never work in the Democratic Party again.

"Tell them to bug off," I said.

But they'd been pressured to quit, and they did. My fund-raiser chose to work for the guy who eventually won. I'd stuck my neck out and had no one to run my campaign. Finally, I found a good conservative campaign strategist, but we had no way to recruit top-level staffers.

In Milwaukee, there are no Republican operatives, and the Democrats refused to work with me. We found a guy in Ohio who was willing to relocate to Wisconsin to help me run. Although I was glad to have his help, he knew nothing about Wisconsin or Milwaukee. My campaign was off to a bad start, and only got worse. I learned a lot about politics through this experience. In politics, trust no one. Listen to strategists with suspicion, because the candidate has skin in the game and the most to lose. If I lose, they pack up their traveling road show and go on to the next money-making opportunity. I am left to sift through the rubble and try to figure out what went wrong, usually by myself. It's a lesson I still remember to this day. Since then, I've passed on two mayoral races, even though influential business leaders begged me to run. In the most recent race, prominent businessmen invited me to breakfast to pitch me to run for mayor. It was a full-court press.

"I'm not interested in running for mayor," I said, "but I'll listen to what you have to say."

"This current mayor isn't getting it done. He's been a disappointment," they said. "What would it take to get you to run?"

"I don't want to lead you on, but if you raise me one million dollars before I announce, I'll consider it."

"We can raise you one million dollars," they promised.

"I've heard that before," I said, remembering how my chief fundraiser Barb Candy left me high and dry on the previous mayoral race. "I want to see it in the bank before I'll even think about it."

About a month passed, and I sat down for lunch with the same group. "Good news," they said. "We have five hundred thousand dollars committed."

"That's not enough," I said. "I said one million dollars. And I don't want verbal commitments, but actual checks. I'll give it back if I don't run."

"We think we can get you another five hundred thousand before the race," they assured me.

"Thanks, I appreciate you guys," I said. "But no thanks."

The Great Big Political Mirage

Politics is a cutthroat business that's all about creating a mirage. Truth doesn't matter, just image. That's why I have no interest in running for elected office other than being sheriff. I'm not running for mayor, I'm not running for congressman, I'm not running for senator, and I'm not running for governor.

That's why I also don't point to elected politicians as the people who are going to save America. I have one Savior—Jesus Christ—and that's all I need. But some voters overestimate a certain candidate and think, *This man might be the one*, or *This woman can certainly bring us out of our national slump*. Though we typically dislike and distrust politicians, we believe *our candidate* is the one who will go to DC and resist the temptations of power. Whenever we're tempted to put this much stock into a human, we should pause a second. When it comes to politics, people sometimes forget their theology and their history.

First, the Bible doesn't paint a very flattering picture of humankind. Romans 3:23 (NKJV) tells us that "*all have sinned* and fall short of the glory of God" (NKJV, emphasis mine). And I have to assume that Psalm 5:9 (ESV) was written specifically for politicians: "For there is no truth in their mouth; *their inmost self is destruction;* their throat is an open grave; they flatter with their tongue" (ESV, emphasis mine).

Second, the Founding Fathers knew this reality of human nature. Alexander Hamilton remarked upon the "folly and wickedness of mankind," and declared that he regarded "human nature as it is, without flattering its virtue or exaggerating its vices." Consequently, he believed "men are ambitious, vindictive, and rapacious." In 1788 James Madison wrote, "There is a degree of depravity in mankind which requires a certain degree of circumspection and distrust." And Thomas Jefferson wrote, "In questions of power, let no more be heard of confidence in man but bind him down from mischief by the chains of the constitution." Supreme Court Chief Justice John Jay believed men were governed by "the dictates of personal interest" and therefore would "swerve from good faith and justice."

One of the most influential books of colonial times was *The New England Primer*, which was first published in 1690. For about fifty years, it was the only textbook in America, and it covered the Lord's Prayer and catechisms, and had a rhyme to teach every letter of the alphabet to schoolchildren. To learn the letter *A*, for example, the textbook taught, "In Adam's fall, we sinned all."

Yes, that was before Americans stopped believing in personal responsibility. These days, no matter what a person does, there's an explanation for the behavior. Is a kid greedy? Well, he was deprived of early childhood education. Is a man lazy? His mother was too demanding. Is a person too fearful? Well, his Little League coach yelled too much. Did a man cheat on his taxes? He was following the rationale that everybody does it. For every behavior, there's a get-out-of-jail-free justification. Modern philosophy means that no one is ever accountable for his or her behavior. But it's time to bring responsibility back in vogue. That's what my dad did with me.

Gonna Take More Than an Election
to Create Real Change

As I mentioned, my father was in the Korean War as a Ranger. After the war, he enjoyed parachuting out of airplanes as a hobby, especially since fewer people were shooting at him. He'd take me with him to watch his recreational jumps. When I was only about eleven years old, he gave me the responsibility of helping him pack his parachute. That is a big responsibility for anyone. It'd be almost unimaginable for a kid these days to have that task. But when your actions could mean life or death, you make sure to get it right. Even when I was a kid, my dad described me as disciplined, meticulous, and competent. Later, when my dad was asked about letting me handle such a responsibility, he laughed and said, "He had every crease and pleat in place."

When you hear the words *kids these days*, it's easy to conjure images of an old man sitting on the front porch yelling when a ball falls in his yard. But I'm not upset at kids these days. I'm upset at parents these days. They either overparent or underparent. Mostly on the job, we see kids who are underparented and neglected. At the other end of the spectrum, overparenting leads to coddling and overindulgence. Here's the thing. People have to take responsibility for themselves. Parents need to take responsibility for their family life, kids have to take responsibility for their futures, and, yes, citizens need to take responsibility for this nation. Part of the citizen responsibility is refusing to be treated like subjects instead of citizens by our federal government.

Have you ever been at a backyard barbecue with the neighbors or at church with fellow congregants when people start complaining about the way this nation is going? It's easy to get people animated when you talk about the federal government's incompetence, overreach, or down-right malice toward average Americans. But when you ask people what they think we should do, there's no easy answer. The late Judge Robert Bork said that we may inevitably complain for a while but then we acquiesce. Some people just throw their hands in the air in exasperation. Others may say, "Well, we need to get together and elect conservatives who will follow the rule of law." That usually gets some nods of approval.

In November 2016, those people sick of government-as-usual

showed up to the polls, shocking those in the political world of punditry who apparently hadn't talked to a normal American in years.

You remember the scene as election night unfolded? The "talking heads" looked as if they were on the verge of tears when having to call states that have historically been "blue" as going "red." CNN was so cautious in calling the states, like they couldn't actually believe what was happening. It's almost as if you could see what was going on in their heads: *What about the polling? I don't know anyone who voted for Trump!* But, when all of the ballots were counted, political shockwaves were sent through the nation: The Republicans, who were supposed to lose, won—and big.

Other than people with the last name "Trump," no one was more excited than I. I'd been traveling non-stop on the campaign trail trying to make sure a Clinton never stepped foot inside the Oval Office again. Even though I am thrilled with the outcome of the 2016 presidential race, I'm here to tell you: *this nation needs more than just an election.*

Every four years, grand promises are made and broken. Every four years, hopeful voters become teary as they watch their favorite candidate place his hand on the Bible and promise to "preserve, protect and defend the Constitution of the United States." I'll admit it. The ceremony is beautiful, and I'm amazed at the peaceful transition of power that occurs at the end of a president's term. But after the balloons deflate, the crowds go home, and actual governing begins, usually not much changes.

I believe Donald Trump is a different type of leader and will keep his promises, but that won't be enough to combat the systematic structural problems that exist in the federal government. He'll need to change the underlying structural problems that somehow let the incompetent federal government bully us with regulations in every aspect of our lives. He'll have to figure out a way to combat the non-elected federal bureaucrats who dictate so many rules and regulations and even target law-abiding, patriotic Americans. He'll still need to prevent future presidents from governing by executive order as did his predecessor, President Barack Obama. He'll still have a Supreme Court that might stubbornly misinterpret the Constitution and legislate from the bench.

That's why "we the people" are going to have to quit saying, "I'll wait for the next election, the next savior, the perfect candidate, the next Ronald Reagan." Nothing will change until the people rise up and declare, "We're not waiting around for Washington, DC, to do it for us." It's pitchfork and torches time in America. The question becomes how do we create the critical mass of Americans to stare down the overreaching federal government? We can tell things have gotten out of hand by looking at the bureaucratic nightmare our government has become.

First, our national debt is currently $19 trillion and growing. Because of Social Security and other entitlement programs, we owe more than an additional $100 million! When you hear politicians complaining that the rich don't pay enough taxes, you have to realize that even if the government took 100 percent of all of our paychecks, we'd still be in debt. In other words, we can't tax ourselves out of this mess. Second, states should have more rights than the federal government recognizes. That is what our Founding Fathers intended. Federal grants have kept states under the federal government's thumb instead of allowing them to be the independent governments they're supposed to be. Third, Congress keeps making more and more laws that regulate business and commerce. Most of those laws cripple large and small businesses alike, slashing productivity and causing Americans to lose jobs. Fourth, the government keeps expanding beyond its regulated parameters. Though the Founders created a checks and balances government composed of three branches, the branches now collude with each other. The power of the states has been so diluted because of this collusion that the federal government is now high on its power.

I've seen it with my own eyes. In May 2015, I testified before a House Judiciary Committee hearing on policing strategies for the twenty-first century. Let's say I was underwhelmed by Obama's blame-the-cop policies. Though I was honored to have been invited by House Judiciary Committee Chairman Bob Goodlatte (R-Va.), I noted that very few of the so-called experts knew anything about policing. A couple of lapdog bureaucrats testified followed by a series of academic elitists. I was more than happy to explain to these pencil pushers how their so-called strategies would play out on the streets. The bureaucrats were just trying to distract, to talk about anything to prevent the public from seeing the real problem of the American ghetto. It's not the American police officer. Modern liberalism has been a wrecking ball on the black community and the black family structure for decades. I told them their strategies were too heavy on federal involvement and control. But even if they were enacted, they wouldn't change the behavior of many law enforcement agencies or the behavior of many individuals of color with whom we come in contact on the streets and end up in deadly confrontations.

Some Orders Aren't Worth Following

Policing is local, and we certainly don't need bureaucrats from on high condescending to us with their meaningless recommendations, policy changes, or mandates. And speaking of mandates, I made headlines when I told former prosecutor and judge Jeanine Pirro that I would not participate in helping the feds compromise states' rights. If the federal government began a gun confiscation program, I'd refuse. (Yes, even if the White House issued an executive order.) Why? For one thing, I wouldn't want to get shot. The American people are only going to put up with so much intervention from the federal government before they push back. If the feds try to disarm this country, you will see the second coming of the American Revolution.

The fact is, most Americans believe the federal government has grown too big and don't want it meddling in our local affairs. Bureaucrats in some dusty Washington, DC. office won't make the decisions those of us close to home would make. Most Americans actually agree on that point. A poll of both Republicans and Democrats had shocking results. According to Washington's Blog:

- 84% of all Americans believe political leaders are more interested in protecting their power and privilege than doing what is right.
- 81% believe the power of ordinary people to control our country is getting weaker every day as politicians of both parties fight to protect their own power and privilege.
- 80% believe the federal government is its own special interest primarily looking out for itself.
- 79% of all voters believe we need to recruit and support more candidates for office, at all levels of government, who are ordinary citizens, rather than professional politicians and lawyers.
- 78% believe that the Democratic and Republican Parties are essentially useless in changing anything, because both political parties are too beholden to special interests to create any meaningful change.

- 76% of Americans agree with the statement that America cannot succeed unless we take on and defeat the corruption and crony capitalism in our government.
- 75% believe that the US government is NOT working for the people's best interest.
- 75% believe that powerful interests have used campaign and lobbying money to rig the system for themselves.
- 74% see the biased and slanted coverage of the media as part of the problem.
- 72% of Americans believe the U.S. has a two-track economy, where most Americans struggle every day, where good jobs are hard to find, and where huge corporations get all the rewards.
- 72% believe that the reason families in our middle class have not seen their economic condition improve for decades and economic growth is stalled is because of corruption and crony capitalism in Washington.
- 71% believe our government is not only dysfunctional, it is collapsing right before our eyes.
- 70% believe the government in Washington does not govern with the consent of the people.
- The majority—56%—say they wish there were a third party with a chance of success to fight for their interests.
- Only 15% say the "values and principals [sic] of my political party are so important that I strongly prefer to vote for the candidates of my party."[1]

Constitutional activist Mark Meckler wrote, "Unless some political force outside of Washington, DC, intervenes, the federal government will continue to bankrupt this nation, embezzle the legitimate authority of the states, and destroy the liberty of the people. Rather than securing the blessings of liberty for future generations, Washington, DC, is on a path that will enslave our children and grandchildren to the debts of the past."[2]

But the question remains. What do you say to your neighbors and friends? What can an average man or woman do to fight back against a government that seems to be spiraling out of control? I look forward to seeing how Trump will go in there and shake things up. But I'm more and more convinced that the necessary solution for permanent change is restricting the size, scope, and power of the federal government by using a tool that the Founders gave us, Article V. The Founders, being the wise people that they were, saw this government overreach coming way back in 1776. They knew one day the federal government would grow so large and powerful that it would never voluntarily give up power.

To combat this inevitability, the Founders gave us a tool that *Forbes* magazine called "a Constitutional emergency cord." The last time you read Article V of the US Constitution may have been in high school, but read it with fresh eyes today:

The Congress, whenever two thirds of both houses shall deem it necessary, shall propose amendments to this Constitution, or, on the application of the legislatures of two thirds of the several states, shall call a convention for proposing amendments, which, in either case, shall be valid to all intents and purposes, as part of this Constitution, when ratified by the legislatures of three fourths of the several states, or by conventions in three fourths thereof, as the one or the other mode of ratification may be proposed by the Congress; provided that no amendment which may be made prior to the year one thousand eight hundred and eight shall in any manner affect the first and fourth clauses in the ninth section of the first

article; and that no state, without its consent, shall be deprived
of its equal suffrage in the Senate.

Most of us were taught one rather difficult way to change the
Constitution: if two-thirds of both houses of Congress agree on an
amendment, Congress can propose it to the Constitution. However,
right there in plain sight is another way—one that does not require the
permission of Congress or even the president. Reread it to see if you
can spot it. I'll wait.

Okay, so did you see it?

The Congress, whenever two thirds of both houses shall deem
it necessary, shall propose amendments to this Constitution, or,
on the application of the legislatures of two thirds of the several
states, shall call a convention for proposing amendments . . .

In addition to going through Congress, our Founding Fathers gave
us—normal, everyday people working through our state legislatures—
the power to dial this out-of-control federal government back: it starts
by passing an application through two-thirds of the state legislatures.
Doing this will force Congress to call a Convention of States where we
can propose amendments that deal with the same issue: taking back the
power from the federal government.

Most Americans don't know that this is a possibility or that the
Founders gave us this power. They certainly don't realize that a committed group of people are already getting these applications passed
through their legislatures. By mid-2016, eight states had passed the
application—Alabama, Alaska, Florida, Georgia, Tennessee, Louisiana,
Oklahoma, and Indiana—and many more are to come.

The actual application looks like this:

CONVENTION *of* STATES ACTION

Application for a Convention of States under
Article V of the Constitution of the United States

Whereas, the Founders of our Constitution empowered State Legislators to be guardians of liberty against future abuses of power by the federal government, and

Whereas, the federal government has created a crushing national debt through improper and imprudent spending, and

Whereas, the federal government has invaded the legitimate roles of the states through the manipulative process of federal mandates, most of which are unfunded to a great extent, and

Whereas, the federal government has ceased to live under a proper interpretation of the Constitution of the United States, and

Whereas, it is the solemn duty of the States to protect the liberty of our people—particularly for the generations to come—by proposing Amendments to the Constitution of the United States through a Convention of States under Article V for the purpose of restraining these and related abuses of power,

Be it therefore resolved by the legislature of the State of _____:

Section 1. The legislature of the State of _____ hereby applies to Congress, under the provisions of Article V of the Constitution of the United States, for the calling of a convention of states limited to proposing amendments to the Constitution of the United States that impose fiscal restraints on the federal government, limit the power and jurisdiction of the federal government, and limit the terms of office for its officials and for members of Congress.

Section 2. The secretary of state is hereby directed to transmit copies of this application to the President and Secretary of the United States Senate and to the Speaker and Clerk of the United States House of Representatives, and copies to the members of the said Senate and House of Representatives from this State; also to transmit copies hereof to the presiding officers of each of the legislative houses in the several States, requesting their cooperation.

Section 3. This application constitutes a continuing application in accordance with Article V of the Constitution of the United States until the legislatures of at least two-thirds of the several states have made applications on the same subject.

That might not be the most exciting thing you've read this week, but it is definitely the most revolutionary. Upholding Article V is the only way things will change. But it will happen only when the states seize their rightful position in this representative democracy. By calling a Convention of States, we can stop the federal spending and debt spree, the power grabs of the federal courts, and other misuses of federal power.

And, yes, I may sound like a Republican, but I'm not one. People often are confused about my political party, and I don't blame them. Usually when you hear a black man talking about politics, he doesn't sound like me. I never joined the Democratic Party, though I ran as a Democrat for the nonpolitical office of sheriff. I didn't want to abandon the party of my family, but the Democratic Party certainly abandoned them and me. I'm a loyal guy but not to a fault. I tell people I'm a conservative. To me, that means the following:

1. Limited government and restrained federal bureaucracy are needed.

2. Military superiority and safe streets at home must be maintained.
3. The rule of law must prevail.
4. The Constitution is about individual rights, not group rights.
5. We need more rights for the states.

The great thing about a Convention of States is that it's not partisan. Americans of all stripes want the federal government to back down. It's going to require hard work to get there. It reminds me of the hard work of parachute packing.

In Vietnam, Captain J. Charles Plumb flew an F-4 Phantom jet on seventy-four successful combat missions. Only five days before he was scheduled to come home, he was shot down, captured, tortured, and imprisoned for 2,103 days as a prisoner of war in a communist prison camp. After he made it home, he was at a restaurant when a young man came up to him and extended his hand. "You're Captain Plumb, right? You're the man who ejected successfully from your F-4 Phantom jet into enemy territory and were a prisoner of war, right?"

"Yes," he said. "But how'd you know all that about me?"

The man responded, "I'm the one who packed your parachute the morning of your capture."

Overcome with gratitude, Captain Plumb asked, "Do you keep track of all the lives you've saved?"

"I don't keep track of all the parachutes I've packed," he responded. "It's enough gratification for me just to know that I served."

His answer left Captain Plumb speechless. Later, he described why he was dumbfounded. "Here's a sailor well below the line of the aircraft carrier. The guy stands at a long wooden table and folds the silks of these parachutes, while the jet jockeys, the *Top Gun* pilots are zooming around the sky at twice the speed of sound. They couldn't have cared less about the guy down there in the hole," he said. "But I cared that day when he packed the parachute for me."[3]

When it comes to life, and even to saving this nation, it comes down to serving others.

I have to believe that Americans share this sailor's desire to do the rather unglamorous work of saving this nation for their kids and grandkids. No, your friends at the barbecue or at church probably won't be on Fox News. They won't be asked to testify at Congress. But the triumph of our Constitution is that ordinary people gave the power to preserve this nation to a group of other ordinary people. Those ordinary folks had the courage and the conviction to defy a king.

Did you know that three times as many colonists supported King George during the Revolution than support our Congress today?

America is a resilient country. It has been through a lot. Think about it a minute. We've been through a revolution, a civil war that nearly tore this country in two. America has been through two World Wars, a Great Depression, and the turbulent 1960s. We've been through 9/11, and we not only survived but came out stronger. Human nature has us believing that this current time is the worst it has ever been. John 14:1 (KJV) reminds us, "Let not your heart be troubled, ye believe in God, believe also in me." I have traveled all over this great country, and I have met Americans of every color, gender, and religion. I have seen the greatness of America in those travels. I believe that America will survive our current challenges because I believe in the ability of American people to overcome anything that confronts us. I feel a revolution coming on. And this time, it will once again come down to ordinary Americans deciding that they've had enough and that freedom and liberty are worth fighting for.

16

War Has Been Declared on the American Police Officer

ON DECEMBER 20, 2014, a call came into the 70th Precinct station house in East Flatbush in the middle of Brooklyn. The call came not from a citizen, but from the Baltimore Police Department. They were concerned after seeing an Instagram post from one of their city's residents, Ismaaiyl Abdullah Brinsley, who'd posted a photo of a silver Taurus pistol with this caption: "I'm Putting Wings on Pigs Today. They Take 1 of Ours . . . Let's Take 2 of Theirs. #ShootThePolice #RIPErivGarner[1] #RIPMikeBrown This may be my final post. I'm putting pigs in a blanket." The post included a gun emoji.

The Baltimore police saw this post at 1:30. Within forty minutes, they'd discovered the twenty-eight-year old Brinsley was heading to New York and consequently alerted the East Flatbush police. Acting quickly, the Flatbush police issued a warning to their officers.

Meanwhile, Brinsley placed his Taurus pistol inside a Styrofoam container and put that container into a plastic bag. Then he boarded a bus that took him to Midtown and then on a subway train to Atlantic Center Mall. There, Brinsley saw a police cruiser at the corner of Tompkins and Myrtle Avenues in Bedford-Stuyvesant. Two partners—forty-year-old Officer Rafael Ramos and thirty-two-year-old Officer Wenjian Liu—were sitting in the cruiser. They wouldn't have time to receive warning from headquarters. At 2:47 p.m., Brinsley walked up to the cruiser and fired his weapon through the front passenger window. He hit both officers in the head. It happened so fast they could not draw their weapons. It's possible they didn't even see him. After this execution-style double murder, Brinsley fled to the Myrtle-Willoughby Avenues subway station and shot himself on the platform.

Lie of the Year

The *Washington Post*'s fact checker awarded 2015's "Lie of the Year" to the "hands up, don't shoot" mantra that spread over the nation like a bad case of flu after the death of Michael Brown. A grand jury in Ferguson refused to indict police officer Darren Wilson because the DNA bloodstain evidence and witness accounts did not support the "hands up, don't shoot" version.

Also, you recall reports of Eric Garner's death were riddled with inaccuracies. When the NYPD approached him illegally selling single cigarettes on the street in Staten Island, they put him in a headlock. "I can't breathe," he said before dying. Counter to prevailing media myth, the medical examiner determined his acute and chronic bronchial asthma, heart disease, and obesity were factors in his death. The windpipe of the four-hundred-pound Garner was not damaged.

After these incidents, you'd think that America's top cop, Attorney General Eric Holder, would be on the side of the police instead of the criminals. However, that wasn't the case. On Tuesday, December 9, 2014, Holder delivered remarks at the My Brother's Keeper Summit in Memphis, Tennessee:

In recent months, with the tragic deaths of Michael Brown, in Ferguson, Missouri, and Eric Garner, in New York City, we've seen the beginning of important national reflection and conversation. These incidents have brought long-simmering divides to the surface. They have sparked widespread public demonstrations. And they have focused a spotlight on the rifts that can develop between police officials and the citizens they are entrusted to serve and protect.

None of these concerns are limited to any one city, state, or geographic region. They are American issues that are truly national in scope. They demand a constructive response from our entire country. And, at their core, they are far larger than just the police and the community—implicating concerns about the fairness of our justice system as a whole, and the persistent opportunity gaps faced by far too many people throughout the nation—and by boys and young men of color in particular . . .

As Attorney General, I have repeatedly made clear that racial profiling by law enforcement is not only wrong, it is misguided and ineffective—because it can mistakenly focus investigative efforts, waste precious resources, and, ultimately, undermine the public trust . . .

Particularly in light of the recent incidents we've seen at the local level—and the widespread concerns, about trust in the criminal justice process, that so many have raised throughout the nation—it's imperative that we take every possible action to ensure strong and sound policing practices. We must instill the absolute highest standards of professionalism and integrity.[2]

Note that on December 9, Holder confirmed the lies of the Black LIES Matter movement, even though there was *no* evidence that these deaths were caused by racial profiling, which has yet to be defined by cop haters. It is one of those nebulous terms that the Left intentionally throws around to incite anger and emotion in black people.

Eric Holder's USDOJ research arm, the National Institute of Justice (NIJ), conducted a study in 2013 of police traffic stop data. The NIJ concluded that "differences in traffic stops can be simply attributed to differences in offending." Additionally, federal data compiled by the National Highway Traffic Safety Administration concluded that "blacks violate traffic laws at higher rates than whites in every offense including driving with an invalid license."

Rather than rely on the findings of the very study he asked for, race provocateur Holder went on a witch hunt to mischaracterize and slander the integrity, honor, courage, character, commitment, and sacrifice that truly define the American police officer.

I was not willing to give Eric Holder the benefit of the doubt after he initially threw law enforcement officers under the bus when emotions were high. When he doubled down on his rhetoric in this speech, however, I became more disgusted by his scurrilous claims that law enforcement officers hit the streets every day with some nefarious intent in their hearts to deny people of their constitutional civil rights and indiscriminately shoot black males as if it's some sort of sport. It was irresponsible for someone in his position to be so dismissive of the actual facts. He knows what due process is and what it looks like. But though he claimed to want "justice for all," apparently that didn't include police officers.

Facts matter. Words have meanings. Ideas have consequences.

Holder knew that, but he wasn't alone in his carelessness. Members of the Congressional Black Caucus said that basically police kill black people with impunity. Representative Hank Johnson, a Democrat from Georgia, said, "It feels like open season on black men in America, and

I'm outraged." This kind of divisive politics extended all the way up to the White House: the fictitious "war on women" pitted men against women; class warfare pitted the wealthy against the poor; the Black LIES Matter rhetoric pitted whites against blacks. Again and again, the liberal elites tried to convince Americans to feel that their enemies were other Americans. That reopened the racial wound, leaving everyone feeling vulnerable.

Eric Holder and Barack Obama are smart men. They know that their words reverberate through the culture. However, they continued to side with the criminals instead of the police . . . to grave results. What happens when you tell Americans that their police are misguided, racist, and irresponsible?

Well, a funny thing. People believe you.

Black Americans began feeling justice wasn't served in cases that involve black people, and they got scared. Actually, they also got mad. After all, it would be a scary thing to think that police were targeting you, right? The facts didn't bear that out. But what happens when political elites pair with media elites and the truth never reaches Americans?

Eleven days after Holder's speech, we found out.

That's when the Baltimore resident decided to take matters into his own hands. In his Instagram, he said exactly why he killed two innocent police officers in cold blood. What's so surprising is not that some malcontent misinterpreted the facts of police shootings but that the attorney general, the president of the United States, congressmen, and the media spread the same lies, misinformation, and distrust.

When I was interviewed after the two officers were shot, I said, "War has been declared on the American police officer." I went on to say, "We might be reaching a tipping point with the mind-set of officers, who are beginning to wonder if the risks they take to keep communities safe are even worth it anymore. In New York and other places, we're seeing a natural recoil from law enforcement officers who don't feel like certain people need to have their backs."

The "certain people" knew I was talking about them—the people who created this fake crisis in the first place, including Cop-Hater-in-Chief Obama. This statement garnered much eye-rolling among the liberal press, but I was too incensed to be diplomatic. I wasn't going to stick my head in the sand about the fact that it's open season right now on cops. Some accused me of using over-the-top rhetoric, but the American police officer knew it instinctively.

New York police union president Pat Lynch knew this. "There is blood on many hands tonight—those that incited violence on the streets under the guise of protest, that tried to tear down what New York police officers did every day," he said. "That blood on the hands starts on the steps of City Hall, in the office of the mayor."

These harsh words were deserved and more. After all, this same mayor said he worried that his (black) son would be safe. "And not just from some of the painful realities of crime and violence in some of our neighborhoods, but safe from the very people they want to have faith in as their protectors."[3] Police officers—both black and white—rightly interpreted these remarks as slams on their professionalism and integrity. Even worse, they believed these remarks created an atmosphere that caused these two officers' deaths. Lynch didn't stop there. "It is your failed policies and actions that enabled this tragedy to occur. I only hope and pray that more of these ambushes and executions do not happen again."

When de Blasio heard the news that the police officers had died, he went to the Woodhull Hospital to pay his respects. The mayor had to go through a hallway filled with grieving officers to reach the families. Many officers silently turned their backs away from the mayor as he passed. It was a chilling moment, but there was more to come.

About twenty-eight thousand people were lined up for blocks along Brooklyn's Sixty-Fifth Street to grieve and honor the memory of Officer Ramos. As de Blasio's image appeared on giant video screens, one cop called out, "About face!"[4] That's how, at the largest NYPD funeral ever, many people sent a loud and clear statement: police officers are sick of careless politicians making us out to be the bad guys.

Police Commissioner Bill Bratton was unhappy about the silent protest at Ramos's funeral and had urged cops not to do it again, but at Officer Liu's memorial, the scene repeated itself.

It was a rainy day—not a driving rain, but more than a mist. The wall of police officers was out the door of the funeral home and extended as far as I could see. I was driven right up to the front, which I felt bad about. Those officers had been waiting in the rain for hours, and I was cutting in front of them to show my respects. I explained that I couldn't stand in line because of a television appearance, and the police officers were super kind. "No, don't worry about it," they said, motioning for me to go inside.

I made my way inside where the body was laid and had the chance to meet Ramos's widow and his sons. It had been a couple weeks since his funeral because many of Officer Liu's family members had to fly in from China. "I'm sorry for your loss," I said to Officer Ramos's widow. It was the only thing I could say. Words couldn't actually convey the grief I was feeling.

I then expressed my condolences to the family sitting in the first row. They had a Chinese-speaking interpreter beside them to help them understand what people were saying. I'm sure people said the same words again and again—*I'm so sorry*.

The interpreter explained who I was to the various family members, and they nodded their heads. His mother hugged me and in broken English thanked me for coming. Then his dad—obviously distraught—shook my hand and wouldn't let it go. I felt bad because I'd skipped the line, and then I was delaying progress. He probably didn't understand what a sheriff was, but we had a moment between us that I'll never forget. As I left, I looked at the thousands of police officers standing outside Aievoli Funeral Home in the rain to pay their respects, and I was overcome by my appreciation for this blue fraternity.

Once again, when the mayor made his remarks, they turned their backs away from a large video feed. Those police officers knew that my "war has been declared on the American police officer" statement was regrettably not hyperbole. History has shown that my prediction has tragically come true.

One of the next battles in this war against the American police officer happened in Dallas. There, during a Black LIES Matter protest, a heavily armed sniper killed five police officers. According to Dallas Police Chief David O. Brown, the shooter told the police during the ensuing standoff that "he was upset about Black Lives Matter. He said he was upset about the recent police shootings. The suspect said he was upset with white people. The suspect stated he wanted to kill white people, especially white officers."[5]

Again, ideas have consequences.

But there was an unintended consequence of this fake race crisis that liberals didn't anticipate: it's getting black people killed. For those of you who work at CNN, here's how that works: When you make the jobs of thousands of police officers more difficult by spreading lies about the profession, it makes police work harder. In cities like Milwaukee, St. Louis, Chicago, and Baltimore, crime is skyrocketing even though it had declined or remained the same for years.

In September 2015, the *New York Times* showed that Milwaukee and St. Louis were on pace for their highest number of murders in more than a decade. Baltimore was recording much the same trajectory. Compared to the same time during the previous year, gun violence in Baltimore was up more than 60 percent; Milwaukee homicides were up 180 percent; in St. Louis, shootings were up 39 percent, robberies 43 percent, and homicides 25 percent.[6] These citywide statistics were staggering. Notably, shootings in one East Harlem precinct were up 500 percent.

The "experts" interviewed by *New York Times* reporters had different explanations for the incredible spikes of violence. They speculated that the increase was due to rivalries in gangs, the ubiquity of guns, a "culture of violence," and drugs. However, none cited evidence that any of these were actually on the rise over previous years.[7]

"The most plausible explanation of the current surge in lawlessness is the intense agitation against American police departments over the past nine months," wrote Heather Mac Donald, who pointed out that murders of police officers rose 89 percent in 2014.[8]

Exactly.

FBI Director James Comey said, "I spoke to officers privately in one big city precinct who described being surrounded by young people with mobile phone cameras held high, taunting them the moment they get out of their cars." He added, "They told me, 'We feel like we're under siege and we don't feel much like getting out of our cars.' I've been told about a senior police leader who urged his force to remember that their political leadership has no tolerance for a viral video."

The Ferguson Effect

Mac Donald called this "chill wind" blowing through law enforcement departments across America the Ferguson Effect, and it's obvious to everyone but liberals. The "experts" in the *New York Times* article ignored the one thing those three cities shared: Black LIES Matter had targeted them with intense scrutiny and criticism. Consequently, fewer arrests were made in St. Louis and Baltimore, and more murders were being committed. (Notice how those two go hand in hand.) In Milwaukee, Police Chief Ed Flynn said that after all of the media and activist push-back surrounding what was deemed as "aggressive" policing techniques, the department decided to focus on "building empathy."

Building empathy? Does Flynn moonlight as a greeting card writer at Hallmark or did he just forget he was chief of police? Either way, he's missing out on a vital understanding of human nature. The criminal underclass is not going to respond well to his overtures. They are predators in search of prey. Passive policing is a recipe to get more cops—and more black people in poorer neighborhoods—killed.

I've not had much respect for Flynn since I saw his true colors. On April 30, 2014, an employee of Starbucks within Red Arrow Park called the police because a guy was lying on a bench outside the entrance. He was either sleeping or passed out and seemed to be a homeless person. Christopher Manney, the beat officer for that section of downtown, responded to the assignment.

Cops are frequently put in situations that don't fit within their core competency or skills set. For example, if a man is acting erratically in the roadway, we send in police. Why are we sending a cop? It seems we might send a mental health professional instead, right? If there's a burglary in progress, that's obviously a mission for the cops. But society is not set up in a way to effectively deal with complicated situations, and the police are sent in. Naturally, their instincts and training kick in and these situations can go sideways fast. This is exactly what happened with Officer Manney.

He carefully approached the man on the bench, not knowing if he'd have to do CPR or be attacked. He got out his nightstick and tried to rouse the man. He helped him up to a sitting position, then to standing on his feet. He started patting the guy down, which is permissible for police to do if there's reasonable suspicion that the guy might have a weapon. Since homeless people are notorious for having weapons—to protect themselves from other homeless people—Officer Manney was well within his right to pat the guy down. The Supreme Court (*Terry v. Ohio 1968*) established this precedent.

While he was patting him down, the guy grabbed the nightstick and started beating the officer over the head with it. He was really bringing it. We later found out the guy, named Dontre Hamilton, was a schizophrenic who'd been kicked out of his home by his family, who feared him. All Officer Manney knew was that he was getting clobbered, and he feared for his life.

The cop pulled out his gun and emptied his magazine into the assailant, and the man died of his wounds.

Why did he empty his entire magazine? I don't know. When you are in a life-or-death situation, the trauma affects your body in certain ways. That's why on-the-scene accounts of the incidents are frequently wrong and confusing. I don't even think Officer Manney realized he'd shot him that many times, but the press had a field day with a "police shoot unarmed man" narrative.

The prosecutor took eight months to make a decision—an unreasonable amount of time to determine the fate of the officer. The whole time Officer Manney was worried about whether he'd get charged, but no one cares about the mental health of the cop. Even worse, in the meantime, Ed Flynn fired Manney.

"Based on the comprehensive internal investigation conducted by the Milwaukee Police Department, I charged Officer Manney with a violation of our Core Value 1.00, Competence, in reference to his out-of-policy contact with Mr. Hamilton which ultimately led to his within-policy use of force," he said. "Based on the totality of the circumstances . . . I signed an order terminating Christopher Manney from his employment with the Milwaukee Police Department earlier today."[9]

Being fired from the police department is like being dishonorably discharged from the military. It's a humiliation from which many never recover. Manney was facing this, even though he'd done nothing wrong. He did what he was trained to do. In all of my years, I've never even heard of an "improper pat down." Even if there was such a thing, that should've been up to the court to determine. Flynn acted before the district attorney reviewing the case ultimately came back and said that Manney *had* acted reasonably. At the end of the day, Flynn sacrificed this guy's career for political expediency, and it was despicable.

Here's what I've learned over the almost four decades that I've been wearing the uniform of my community. Police are not perfect. That doesn't come as a news flash to most of you, but the Black LIES Matter crowd needs to be reminded: police don't have to be perfect; we have to be excellent. I repeat *excellent*, not perfect. Most officers reach excellence every day, but—humanity being the way it is—perfection is an unobtainable goal. Even though our police forces are comprised of just ordinary human beings, take a hard look at American police officers if you want to see how society can improve over the years. In the 1950s and '60s, police were turning dogs and fire hoses onto truly peaceful protestors. But we changed. We changed ourselves. Today, we are more professional, more educated, and better trained than in any time in our history. Sadly, self-serving politicians want to transform this profession into something we're not: social workers.

We didn't create the tinderbox of cultural problems that are rampant throughout cities. Failed urban policy has led to the rise of an underclass, defined by generational poverty, government dependency, fatherless homes, failing schools, and questionable lifestyle choices. The government props up an underclass that takes property by force, settles disputes by violence, and refuses to raise its kids.

Police walk the beat in an already simmering situation. Police officers are not responsible for this, and elected officials know it.

I have had enough. I'm not going to let people who have not been a cop one day in their lives try to transform us. It'd be like me trying to reform the medical community after a botched surgery. By the way, did you know medical errors killed 250,000 people in 2014, yet Barack Obama has not put together a task force with a charge of completely transforming the medical profession? In that same year 990 people were killed in police use-of-force incidents. This is not to downplay the number of people killed in police interactions; it is meant to demonstrate the political hyperbole that the police are killing too many people. No, hospital procedures are.

Has the Left demanded the medical community reform its ways? Black LIES Matter? The attorney general? Have you seen protestors block traffic and make signs? Weren't some of those people black? Don't more people die in this manner than at the hands of bad cops? Of course. The government in the United States gets few things right, but one of them is policing.

Sometimes people accuse me of being bombastic or over the top. For example, when I say Obama hates cops, people usually interrupt me and say, "You don't really believe that, do you?" I'm here to tell you that I don't speak carelessly. Facts back up everything I say.

And here's just one fact that tells me Obama hates cops.

Earlier in this chapter, I told you about the assassination of New York Police Department Officers Wenjian Liu and Rafael Ramos. The police in Baltimore were alerted to a possible threat coming to Manhattan, but the officers didn't receive the notice before they were gunned down. After their murders, cop supporters proposed the Rafael Ramos and Wenjian Liu National Blue Alert Act of 2015—a nationwide alert system similar to an Amber Alert. While the Amber Alert notifies people of missing children, the National Blue Alert signals police of possibly dangerous threats to law enforcement. This instantaneous relay of information could help save lives.

In a rare show of nonpartisan support, the legislation sailed through both houses of Congress on a voice vote. The Obama administration signed the bill into law on May 19, 2015—just six months after Liu and Ramos were killed. So how has the new process worked? Has it saved lives?

No. Even though it was signed into law more than a year ago, it has not been enacted. Why?

Twenty-seven states have already implemented a similar system, yet the federal government's implementation has languished in a sea of bureaucratic red tape. The Obama Justice Department bureaucrats say they haven't implemented the program because they can't figure out which office of the Department of Justice should implement it.

Really?

Now, let's do a thought experiment. What if this proposal had to do with punishing officers for their bias against black Americans? How long would it have taken the president to put that into place? He wouldn't have waited for it to pass through Congress before mandatory enactment. It would've been an executive order.

The Obama administration has not made the full implementation an absolute priority because no one there cares about police officers. Obama is a cop hater, someone who will not act to save lives even when a widely supported, uncontroversial bill comes across his desk.

It's inexcusable.

Why I Fight for Police Officers

Recently, I was in Washington, DC, and I did what I always try to do when I'm in the nation's capital. I stopped by the 400 block of East Street NW where the National Law Enforcement Memorial honors law enforcement officers who've made the ultimate sacrifice. The grounds are kept nicer than a golf course, with thick, plush grass, trees, and ten thousand daffodils that bloom in the spring. The center plaza features a bronze medallion with a blue shield that has a red rose draped across it. The two entrances leading to the walls of remembrance are adorned with four powerful groupings of bronze statues—an adult lion protecting its cubs—symbolizing the protective role of law enforcement officers. Under each statue is a quote that points to the valor of the officers who have died.

It is not how these officers died that made them heroes, it is how they lived.

—Vivian Eney Cross, Survivor

In valor there is hope.

—Tacitus

The wicked flee when no man pursueth: but the righteous are bold as a lion.

—Proverbs 28:1

Carved on these walls is the story of America, of a continuing quest to preserve both democracy and decency, and to protect a national treasure that we call the American dream.

—President George H. W. Bush

I stood there by myself, looking at the massive, curving blue-gray marble walls. Twenty thousand names are etched into those two walls, beginning with the first known officer death in 1791. Regrettably, new names are added each spring. Too many names on the cold walls.

Those walls talk to me. I hear them whispering the names of people with whom I've worked, the names of people from Wisconsin who've paid that sacrifice. The names of fathers and mothers. Sons and daughters.

There but for the grace of God go I.

Silence. Deafening, chilling, grief-inducing silence.

When I talk to surviving family members, I think of those walls. When I look at a spouse of a fallen officer, I think of my spouse. When I talk to the siblings, my heart breaks. What must they think as this profession is tarred and feathered?

That's why I decided to fight back. Someone needs to stand up and push back against this false narrative about the American police officer. I don't speak for every officer, but after thirty-eight years, I can *and will* speak for this profession.

That's my mission right now, and I won't stop until this subversive, anarchist, hateful movement dies the ideological death it deserves. Police officers have the overwhelming support of the communities. Changing us into something we're not will get cops and civilians killed.

Stand with me. I'll do the heavy lifting. I'm a fighter. I'll fight to the death if I have to. It's the only way I know.

ACKNOWLEDGMENTS

I NEVER KNEW how many people it takes to write a book. I happened to undertake this book project while Donald J. Trump was running for president and had the honor of going around the country to emphasize the "law and order" aspect of his campaign. That couldn't have happened without many people surrounding me and helping me make life work during that busy time of life.

First, I'd like to thank my talented and tenacious writer, Nancy French, as well as the people at Worthy Publishing. All of them helped shape my thoughts into something that could actually be put between two covers and placed on the shelf: Byron Williamson, Jeana Ledbetter, Kyle Olund, Betty Woodmancy, Dale Wilsterman, Leeanna Nelson, Nicole Pavlas, Caroline Green, Bart Dawson, Ramona Wilkes, David Howell, and Susan Thomas. I'd also like to thank my literary agent D.J. Snell for his constant support.

Second, I'd like to thank Eric O'Keefe for having a vision for this book and helping make it happen.

Third, I'd like to thank my parents, who understood the value of an education and poured what little money they had into providing me with a solid educational base. They knew that in a sometimes unfair and unjust world I would have to be doubly-prepared to overcome obstacles. You were always there for me—checking up on me when I was trying to get away with stuff, taking my shoes during the nights to remove the temptation to sneak out, teaching me responsibility and patriotism as I grew from a kid into a man. I don't say this to you directly in real life, so let me take the opportunity to do it here: this book is a testimony to your good parenting, your selfless provision, and your love.

Fourth, I'd like to thank my executive assistant, Dawn Colla. A proofreader extraordinaire, she has been with me every step of the way. She has a way of detecting mistakes I've never seen, even after having read it three or four times. I've told her she should have been an English teacher, but I'm really glad she wasn't. I'm not sure how I could've done my job without her by my side.

Last but not least I want to thank my wife, Julie. You have been a steadying force during the writing of this book, just as you've ben throughout our whole marriage. Your patience, love, and encouragement have allowed me to accomplish things I otherwise would only be able to dream of. You epitomize the saying "Beside every man who accomplishes great things in life stands a woman who deserves sainthood." I can only hope to return to you in your endeavors what you have done in mine.

NOTES

Chapter 1

1. http://secondrangerinfantrycompany.com/preface.htm
2. Rick Atkinson, *The Day of Battle: The War in Sicily and Italy, 1943–1944*. Vol. 2, The Liberation Trilogy (New York: Henry Holt, 2007), 7635.

Chapter 2

1. Kurt Chandler, "The New Black Power," July 25, 2003 (milwaukeemag.com).
2. Georgia Pabst, "Bloomberg's PAC enters Milwaukee County sheriff's race," August 8, 2014 (jsonline.com).

Chapter 3

1. Thomas Frank, "High-speed police chases have killed thousands of innocent bystanders," July 30, 2015 (usatoday.com).
2. G. P. Alpert, U.S. Department of Justice, National Institute of Justice, Pursuit Management Task Force Report (Washington, DC, 1998), found here: http://www.realpolice.net/articles/police-pursuits/high-speed-police-pursuits-dangers-dynamics-and-risk-reduction.html.
3. Jessica Guynn, "Meet the woman who coined #BlackLivesMatter," March 4, 2015 (usatoday.com).
4. Jay Caspian Kang, "Our Demand Is Simple: Stop Killing Us," May 4, 2015 (nytimes.com).
5. Guynn, "Meet the woman who coined #BlackLivesMatter."
6. Garza, "A Herstory of the #BlackLivesMatter Movement," October 7, 2014 (thefeministwire.com).
7. Michael Walsh, "The myth of the killer-cop 'epidemic,'" January 2, 2016 (nypost.com).
8. Kimberly Kindy, Marc Fisher, Julie Tate, and Jennifer Jenkins, "A Year of Reckoning: Police Fatally Shoot Nearly 1,000," December 26, 2015 (washingtonpost.com).
9. David French, "The Numbers Are In: Black Lives Matter Is Wrong about Police," December 29, 2015 (nationalreview.com).
10. Walsh, "The myth of the killer-cop 'epidemic,'" (nypost.com).
11. Bill Kauffman, "Freedom Now II: Interview with Clarence Thomas," November 1987 (reason.com).
12. Dustin Block and Jeff Wilford, "Excessive force used after high-speed chase, local NAACP leader alleges," January 10, 2003 (journaltimes.com).

Chapter 4

1. http://county.milwaukee.gov/ImageLibrary/Groups/cntySheriff/sheriffnews/2013-New/081913Abelerunsfromhisresponsi.pdf
2. Final Report: A Focused Review of the Milwaukee County Correctional Center-South; National Institute of Corrections; Technical Assistance #10J1013; December 20, 2009; Jeffrey A. Schwartz.
3. Raquel Rutledge, "Hold the jelly—or the bread," May 2, 2008 (jsonline.com).
4. Ibid.

5. Ibid.

6. Jim Stingl, "Breaking Nutraloaf out of the big house—to my house," January 19, 2003 (jsonline.com).

7. http://wi.findacase.com/research/wfrmDocViewer.aspx/xq/fac.20120813_0000700.EWI.htm/qx

8. Ibid.

9. Eliza Barclay, "Food As Punishment: Giving U.S. Inmates 'The Loaf' Persists," January 2, 2014 (npr.org).

10. Jeffrey Toobin, "The Milwaukee Experiment," May 11, 2015 (newyorker.com).

11. Ibid.

12. http://www4.uwm.edu/eti/2013/BlackImprisonment.pdf

13. Jeremy Diamond, "Bill Clinton concedes role in mass incarceration," May 7, 2015 (cnn.com).

14. Aviva Shen, "Hillary Clinton Says She Agrees Her Role in Mass Incarceration Was a Mistake," March 6, 2016 (thinkprogress.org).

15. "Remarks by the President at the NAACP Conference," July 14, 2015 (whitehouse.gov).

16. Michelle Alexander, *The New Jim Crow: Mass Incarceration in the Age of Colorblindness* (New York: The New Press, 2012), 11.

17. http://www.manhattan-institute.org/sites/default/files/IB-HM-0716.pdf

18. Ibid.

19. "Remarks by the President at the NAACP Conference, July 14, 2015 (whitehouse.gov).

20. https://www.judiciary.senate.gov/download/10-19-15-mac-donald-testimony

Chapter 5

1. https://archive.org/details/americanslavecod00lcgood

2. http://literacy.rice.edu/thirty-million-word-gap

3. Ibid.

4. "Parenting in America," December 17, 2015 (pewsocialtrends.org).

5. Lawrence J. Fedewa, "FEDEWA: American schools are failing!" June 1, 2014 (washingtontimes.com).

6. http://mps.milwaukee.k12.wi.us/en/District/About-MPS/Departments/Office-of-Finance/Budget --Finance.htm

7. Timothy Benson, "About Charter Schools, the NAACP Is Simply Wrong," August 26, 2016 (nationalreview.com).

8. Dr. Julian Vasquez Heilig, "Breaking News: @NAACP calls for national moratorium on charters," July 29, 2016 (cloakinginequity.com).

9. Benson, "About Charter Schools."

10. Thomas Sowell, "The Role of 'Educators,'" January 8, 2013 (nationalreview.com).

Chapter 6

1. https://www.documentcloud.org/documents/326700-full-transcript-zimmerman.html

2. Rich Lowry, "A Morality Tale That Failed," July 12, 2013 (nationalreview.com).

3. Richard Luscombe, "George Zimmerman prosecutors have proved his innocence, says lawyer," July 12, 2013 (theguardian.com).

4. https://donate.naacp.org/news/entry/naacp-petition-to-doj-reaches-1.5-million-signatures

5. Dave Boyer, "Obama says police training needed to reduce their racial 'bias,'" January 22, 2015 (washingtontimes.com).

6. Jon Campbell, "Smuggled, Untaxed Cigarettes Are Everywhere in New York City," April 7, 2015 (villagevoice.com).

7. Jack Dunphy, "Officers Did Not Use Excessive Force in Arresting Garner," December 5, 2014 (nationalreview.com).

Chapter 7

1. Erik Eckholm and Matt Apuzzo, "Darren Wilson Is Cleared of Rights Violations in Ferguson Shooting," March 4, 2015 (nytimes.com).
2. John Bacon, "Darren Wilson: Ferguson made me unemployable," August 4, 2015 (usatoday.com).
3. http://blacklivesmatter.com/guiding-principles/
4. Garza, "A Herstory of the #BlackLivesMatter Movement," (thefeministwire.com).
5. John Perazzo, "The Profound Racism of 'Black Lives Matter,'" June 1, 2015 (frontpagemag.com).
6. Opal Tometi, "Black Future Month: Examining the Current State of Black Lives and Envisioning Where We Go from Here," February 1, 2015 (huffingtonpost.com).
7. https://policy.m4bl.org/end-war-on-black-people/
8. https://policy.m4bl.org/reparations/
9. Ibid.
10. Ibid.
11. Ibid.

Chapter 8

1. http://query.nytimes.com/gst/abstract.html?res=980DE7DF133AEF3BBC4D52DFB0668382679E DE&legacy=true
2. "Ex-Black Panther convicted of murder," March 9, 2002 (cnn.com).
3. Details about the funeral service taken from https://news.google.com/newspapers?nid=348&dat =20000322&id=uptOAAAAIBAJ&sjid=6UQDAAAAIBAJ&pg=5391,7671388&hl=en
4. David Firestone, "Ex-Black Militant Gets Life for Murdering Deputy," March 14, 2002 (nytimes.com).
5. "Man indicted for 1971 cop killing," July 14, 2002 (onlineathens.com).
6. Philip Messing, "NYPD Nabs Man Sought in '71 Atlanta Cop Slay," July 17, 2002 (nypost.com).
7. "Police Union: Keep Men Locked Up in 1971 Murders of NYPD Officers," January 23, 2014 (newyork.cbslocal.com).
8. David French, "Black Lives Matter: Radicals Using Moderates to Help Tear America Apart," July 11, 2016 (nationalreview.com).
9. Matt Wilstein, "The 5 Biggest Revelations from *GQ*'s Don Lemon Profile," April 21, 2015 (mediaite.com).

Chapter 9

1. Ed Morrissey, "Video: Milwaukee County sheriff's PSA on self-protection," January 26, 2013 (hotair.com).
2. Linda Greenhouse, "Justices Rule Police Do Not Have a Constitutional Duty to Protect Someone," June 28, 2005 (nytimes.com).
3. Peter Kasler, "Police Have No Duty to Protect Individuals," 1992 (firearmsandliberty.com).
4. *Guns, Murders, and the Constitution* (Pacific Research Institute for Public Policy, 1990).
5. Both George Washington and Samuel Adams quotes: Steve Straub, "Famous Pro-Gun 'Quotes' the Founding Fathers Never Actually Said," (thefederalistpapers.org).
6. https://www.monticello.org/site/research-and-collections/exercise
7. http://foundersquotes.com/founding-fathers-quote/the-constitutions-of-most-of-our-states-assert -that-all-power-is-inherent-in-the-people/
8. See Carrying Concealed Weapons, 15 Va L. Reg. 391, 391-92 (1909).
9. Martin Luther King Jr., *Stride Toward Freedom* (Boston: Beacon Press, 1958), 86.
10. Charles C. W. Cooke, "Do Black People Have Equal Gun Rights?" October 25, 2014 (nytimes.com).
11. https://www.scribd.com/document/50079133/Collected-Works-of-Mahatma-Gandhi-Vol-008

12. Christopher Ingraham, "The shocking difference in how blacks and whites are killed by guns," December 18, 2015 (washingtonpost.com).

Chapter 10

1. Cheryl Wetzstein, "Census: More first-time mothers give birth out of wedlock," July 8, 2014 (washingtontimes.com).
2. Louis Jacobson, "CNN's Don Lemon says more than 72 percent of African-American births are out of wedlock," July 29, 2013 (politifact.com).
3. Tommy Christopher, "Tweetnado: MSNBC's Goldie Taylor Calls Don Lemon a 'Turn Coat Mofo,'" July 27, 2013 (mediaite.com).
4. Annie Lowrey, "Can Marriage Cure Poverty?" February 4, 2014 (nytimes.com).
5. Robert Rector and Rachel Sheffield, "The War on Poverty After 50 Years," September 15, 2014 (heritage.org).
6. Roland Warren, "The Important Lesson the 'Roots' Miniseries Taught Me About Fatherhood," September 12, 2016 (sixseeds.patheos.com).
7. http://www.gphistorical.org/mlk/mlkspeech/mlk-gp-speech.pdf

Chapter 11

1. http://caselaw.lp.findlaw.com/data2/circs/7th/081515p.pdf
2. Ibid.
3. Barronelle Stutzman, "Why a friend is suing me: the Arlene's Flowers story," November 12, 2015 (seattletimes.com).
4. "ACLU file suit for gay couple discriminated against by florist," April 18, 2013 (aclu-wa.org).
5. David French, "Thanks to SCOTUS, Vicious Anti-Christian State Action Is Legal in the Ninth Circuit," June 28, 2016 (nationalreview.com).
6. Ibid.
7. Cheryl Wetzstein, "Ex-fire chief Kelvin Cochran wrongful-firing case to proceed," December 16, 2015 (washingtontimes.com).
8. David French, "How the Atlanta Fire Chief's Christian Views Cost Him His Job," February 25, 2016 (nationalreview.com).
9. Ibid.

Chapter 12

1. http://media.jrn.com/documents/Mass+Shooting+-+Milwaukee-edited.pdf
2. Paul Sperry, "900 'homegrown' ISIS cases being investigated in US: FBI," November 22, 2015 (nypost.com).
3. Kayla Brandon, "Giuliani Makes Powerful Surprise Appearance at Values Summit: US 'More in Danger Today Than on 9/11,'" August 2016 (ijr.com).
4. "FBI, Justice: El Al attack was terrorism," April 12, 2003 (cnn.com).
5. Jennifer Sullivan, "Seattle Jewish center shooter gets life sentence," January 15, 2010 (latimes.com).
6. Ibid.
7. Richard A. Serrano, "Federal government isn't touching Arkansas terrorism case," July 11, 2011 (latimes.com).
8. "I Was There: Boston Marathon Bombings—The Man in the Cowboy Hat," (history.com); "Boston Marathon Terror Attack Fast Facts," April 8, 2016 (cnn.com): number of wounded varies from 170 to 264 depending on source.
9. Timothy Williams and Michael S. Schmidt, "Oklahoma Man Is Charged in Beheading of Co-Worker," September 30, 2014 (nytimes.com).

10. Nick Allen, "Fort Hood gunman had told US military colleagues that infidels should have their throats cut," November 8, 2009 (telegraph.co.uk).

11. Christopher Hitchens, "Hard Evidence," November 16, 2009 (slate.com).

12. David French, "A Few Thoughts on Fort Hood," April 3, 2014 (nationalreview.com).

13. Mattea Kramer and Chris Hellman, "'Homeland Security': The Trillion-Dollar Concept That No One Can Define," February 28, 2013 (thenation.com).

14. David French, "Three Ways the Fort Hood Shooting Previewed Benghazi," August 14, 2013 (nationalreview.com).

Chapter 13

1. Mark Price, "Man arrested for berating Trump backer for 2 hours on flight to Charlotte," September 27, 2016 (charlotteobserver.com).

2. Drew Griffin, Kathleen Johnston, and Todd Scwarzschild, "Sources: Air marshals missing from almost all flights," March 25, 2008 (cnn.com).

3. Debbie Schlussel, "Attention, Terrorists: Over 99% of U.S. Flights Have No Air Marshal; Thanks, Chertoff!" March 25, 2008 (debbieschlussel.com).

4. Everett Potter, "Five myths about air marshals," August 10, 2014 (usatoday.com).

5. Senator Tom Coburn (US Senate, 113th Congress), "A Review of the Department of Homeland Security's Missions and Performance," January 2015; link embedded in article by Ryan Lovelace, "Where Have All the Air Madshals gone?" March 4, 2015 (nationalreview.com).

Chapter 14

1. Chris Cillizza, "Stephen A. Smith wants all black people to vote Republican in 2016. Um, okay." March 19, 2015 (washingtonpost.com).

2. Nate Scott, "Stephen A. Smith wants every black American to vote Republican in one election," March 19, 2015 (usatoday.com).

3. Kay S. Hymowitz, "The Black Family: 40 Years of Lies," Summer 2005 (city-journal.org).

4. Rector and Sheffield, "The War on Poverty After 50 Years" (heritage.org).

5. President Lyndon Johnson, quoted in David Zaretsky, *President Johnson's War on Poverty: Rhetoric and History* (Tuscaloosa: University of Alabama Press, 1986), 49. Taken from: http://www.heritage.org/research/reports/2014/09/the-war-on-poverty-after-50-years#_ftn19

6. "LBJ's 'War on Poverty' Hurt Black Americans," January 8, 2014 (nationalcenter.org).

7. Robert Rector, "Robert Rector: How the War on Poverty Was Lost," January 7, 2014 (wsj.com).

8. Thomas A. Johnson, "Lost Opportunity for Rights Cited," February 9, 1967 (nytimes.com).

9. Malcolm X and Alex Haley, *The Autobiography of Malcolm X* (New York: Grove Press, 1966), 272.

Chapter 15

1. "Overwhelming Majority of Americans Believe that Both Parties Are Too Corrupt to Change Anything . . . 'This, in Fact, Is a Revolution,'" February 8, 2016 (washingtonsblog.com).

2. http://www.conventionofstates.com/problem

3. https://www.youtube.com/watch?v=k2t0E-yaHNs

Chapter 16

1. He spelled "Eric" incorrectly in the original hashtag.

2. https://www.justice.gov/opa/speech/attorney-general-eric-holder-delivers-remarks-my-brothers-keeper-summit-closing-session

3. Douglas Ernst, "De Blasio has 'blood on the hands' after NYPD shooting, says union president," December 21, 2014 (washingtontimes.com).

4. Larry Celona, Shawn Cohen, and Bruce Golding, "Cops ignore Bratton, turn backs on de Blasio at officer's funeral," January 4, 2015 (nypost.com).

5. Manny Fernandez, Richard Pérez-Peña, and Jonah Engel Bromwich, "Five Dallas Officers Were Killed as Payback, Police Chief Says," July 8, 2016 (nytimes.com).

6. Heather Mac Donald, "The New Nationwide Crime Wave," May 29, 2015 (wsj.com).

7. Monica Davey and Mitch Smith, "Murder Rates Rising Sharply in Many U.S. Cities," August 31, 2015 (nytimes.com).

8. Mac Donald, "The New Nationwide Crime Wave."

9. Cary Docter, "COMPLETE STATEMENT: Police Chief Ed Flynn addresses firing of officer in Hamilton case," October 15, 2014 (fox6now.com).

ABOUT THE AUTHOR

Milwaukee County Sheriff DAVID A. CLARKE JR. is a law enforcement executive with 38-plus years of experience. His public service career began in 1978, at the Milwaukee Police Department (MPD), where he served 24 distinguished years. During his 11 years as a Patrol Officer, he received meritorious citations for felony arrests. In 1989, he was promoted to Detective, and 9 months later was selected for the specialized Homicide Division, where he was part of a team that investigated more than 400 homicides in a 4-year period. MPD made arrests in more than 80 percent of homicides, well above the national average of 60 percent.

Clarke was promoted in 1992 to Lieutenant of Detectives and was assigned to the Criminal Investigation Bureau as Shift Commander of the Crimes Against Property Division, the Violent Crimes Unit, and again to the Homicide Division. In 1996, he was promoted to MPD's command staff as Captain of Police, and soon became Commander of the Department's First District, located in Milwaukee's downtown business and entertainment center.

In 1999, Clarke became Commanding Officer of MPD's Intelligence Division, which was responsible for producing and sharing intelligence, and providing dignitary protection in conjunction with the Secret Service, the Department of State, and other federal agencies. He served as MPD's liaison with the United States Attorney's Office as coordinator of the CEASEFIRE violent crime reduction program, and the Federal Bureau of Investigation, Customs Service, Wisconsin Department of Criminal Investigation, the Immigration and Naturalization Service, and the Bureau of Alcohol, Tobacco, and Firearms.

In November 2002, he was elected to his first 4-year term as sheriff of Milwaukee County, earning 64 percent of the vote. Sheriff Clarke is now in his fourth term, having been re-elected in November 2006, 2010, and 2014, increasing his victory margins to 73 percent, 74 percent, and 79 percent, respectively.

Clarke graduated summa cum laude from Concordia University Wisconsin with a degree in Criminal Justice Management, and in May 2003, Concordia honored him with their Alumnus of the Year Award. Sheriff Clarke is a graduate of the FBI National Academy in Quantico, Virginia. This prestigious school trains law enforcement executives from all over the world and provides management and leadership instruction. In July 2004, he completed an intensive three-week Program for Senior Executives in State and Local Government, at Harvard University's John F. Kennedy School of Government.

In October 2004, Sheriff Clarke participated in the 80-hour Executive Development Program of the National Sheriffs' Institute, sponsored by the National Sheriffs' Association and the National Institute of Corrections in Colorado. Clarke returned to Harvard University's John F. Kennedy School of Government in April 2005, to complete the week-long executive education program entitled "Driving Government Performance: Leadership Strategies That Produce Results."

Sheriff Clarke was nominated in 2005 to the FBI's 28th Annual National Executive Institute, a world-renowned leadership development forum for law enforcement executives conducted by recognized experts in leadership, media, ethics, international policies, intelligence-led policing, homeland security, and social, political, and economic trends. The forums were conducted in weeklong cycles in Quantico, Gettysburg, and Ottawa.

In 2009, Sheriff Clarke met with Police Chief William Bratton and Los Angeles County Sheriff Lee Baca to study their operations in Los Angeles. Of special concentration were LAPD's CompStat system, a crime control and analysis model; and LASD's detention services, large jail management, and emergency management operations. He met again with Commissioner Bratton in March 2015, and surveyed NYPD intelligence and counterterrorism operations.

In October 2009, Sheriff Clarke was honored to receive the Americanism Award from the Milwaukee County War Memorial Veterans Board of Directors at their annual awards ceremony. The board, consisting of 22 veteran organizations, historically has awarded civic leaders and community volunteers, and not elected officials. However, board members said they chose to recognize Sheriff Clarke in "appreciation for his version of law and order."

Sheriff Clarke, along with a dozen American police chiefs and sheriffs, traveled to Israel in April 2011, on a week-long law enforcement executive training mission sponsored by the American Israel Education Foundation. They exchanged best practices in areas including airport security, intelligence analysis and sharing, public spaces security, bomb disposal, border security, incident and media management, the psychology of terror, and terror financing.

Sheriff Clarke was honored in May 2013 with the Sheriff of the Year Award from the Constitutional Sheriffs and Peace Officers Association for "demonstrating true leadership and courage . . . staying true to his oath, true to his badge, and true to the people he has promised to serve and protect."

In September 2013, after completing a rigorous master's degree program, Sheriff Clarke received an M.A. in Security Studies from the

U.S. Naval Postgraduate School, Center for Homeland Defense and Security, in Monterey, California. The competitive 18-month program included 12 weeks of in-residence study, course work, on-line study, and the completion of a thesis. As a postgraduate student, Clarke collaborated with national security officials on current policy, strategy, and organizational design challenges in security studies, homeland security, and defense. His thesis analyzed the need to balance domestic intelligence operations with protection of privacy and civil liberties.

In February 2015, the Conservative Political Action Conference presented Sheriff Clarke with the Charlton Heston Courage Under Fire Award. CPAC only presents the award, in years when it deems it is merited, to an individual "who stands up for their principles, even when doing so puts them at risk physically, politically, or economically."

At the request of committee chairmen, Sheriff Clarke testified in January 2015 at the U.S. Senate Judiciary Committee hearing on the confirmation of Loretta Lynch as Attorney General, and at a hearing in May 2015 of the House Committee on the Judiciary regarding "Policing Strategies for the 21st Century."

In November 2015, Sheriff Clarke was presented with the Annie Taylor Award from the David Horowitz Freedom Center for "Daring the Odds." The award is named for Annie Edson Taylor, who was a 63-year-old schoolteacher in 1901, when she became the first person to go over Niagara Falls in a barrel and survive. The Annie Taylor Award is given to people who exhibit great courage by "going over the ledge when others would be afraid to even go near it."

2016 awards include: Law Enforcement Leader of the Year from the Federal Law Enforcement Officers Association; *New Jersey Blue NOW* magazine for Sheriff Clarke's "leadership and support to our nation's law enforcement community"; Sheriff Buford Pusser National Law Enforcement Officer of the Year; New York Oath Keepers Leadership

Award; New York City Patrolmen's Benevolent Association Person of the Year; American Police Hall of Fame George Washington Second Amendment Gun Rights Award; and Massachusetts Police Association Chief Paul Doherty Award.

Sheriff Clarke is a frequent guest commentator for national news services and organizations regarding law enforcement, Second Amendment, and homeland security issues, and has been interviewed by CBS Evening News, CNN (CNN Newsroom with Brooke Baldwin and Poppy Harlow, Michael Smerconish, Don Lemon, and Erin Burnett OutFront), Fox News (Fox & Friends, Sean Hannity, Judge Jeanine Pirro, Megyn Kelly, Bill O'Reilly, Neil Cavuto, Uma Pemmaraju), Fox Business (Lou Dobbs and Charles Payne), Glenn Beck, National Public Radio, *The Washington Times*, *The Washington Post*, *Washington Examiner*, *Politico.com*, Al Jazeera America, National Rifle Association, NRA News, The Heritage Foundation, Conservative Political Action Conference, *National Review* (cover story), *Sheriff*, *America's 1st Freedom* (cover story), and *Concealed Carry*. The Sheriff hosts "*The People's Sheriff*," a weekly one-hour podcast on The Blaze Radio Network.

Sheriff Clarke is a member of several professional organizations, including the American Jail Association, International Association of Chiefs of Police, Major County Sheriffs' Association, Badger State Sheriffs' Association, Milwaukee County Law Enforcement Executives Association, and the National Sheriffs' Association, serving on its Legal Affairs Committee.

He is an Honorary Chair of the Milwaukee Fellowship Open, a member of the Law Enforcement Assistance and Outreach Committees of the National Rifle Association, and a member of the Board of Directors of the Crime Prevention Research Center. Past board memberships include the Three Harbors Council Boy Scouts of America,

Milwaukee Tennis & Education Foundation, Boys & Girls Clubs of Greater Milwaukee, and the American Red Cross in Southeastern Wisconsin.

Sheriff Clarke is a lifelong resident of the city of Milwaukee. A Marquette University High School graduate, he was a proud member of the varsity basketball team that won the state private school championship in 1973. Sheriff Clarke and his wife, Julie Clarke, a Realtor, live in the home they built on the northwest side of Milwaukee.

IF YOU ENJOYED THIS BOOK, WILL YOU CONSIDER SHARING THE MESSAGE WITH OTHERS?

Mention the book in a blog post or through Facebook, Twitter, Pinterest, or upload a picture through Instagram.

Recommend this book to those in your small group, book club, workplace, and classes.

Head over to facebook.com/MilwaukeeCountySheriffDavidAClarkeJr, "LIKE" the page, and post a comment as to what you enjoyed the most.

Tweet "I recommend reading #CopUnderFire by @SheriffClarke // @worthypub"

Pick up a copy for someone you know who would be challenged and encouraged by this message.

Write a book review online.

WORTHY® PUBLISHING

Visit us at worthypublishing.com

twitter.com/worthypub

worthypub.tumblr.com

facebook.com/worthypublishing

pinterest.com/worthypub

instagram.com/worthypub

youtube.com/worthypublishing